Department of Education and Science

Quality in Schools: the Initial Training of Teachers

A survey of initial teacher training in the public sector in England, Northern Ireland and Wales

Carried out by HMI and the Inspectorate in Northern Ireland

January 1983 to January 1985

London: Her Majesty's Stationery Office

ISBN 0 11 270608 8

Contents

Page

PART I
Principal findings and issues arising

1 The task of the teacher: a background to training

The training of a teacher is a complex undertaking, and one that should be seen as a continuous process occupying the full span of professional life. Building on what the students bring with them, good initial training sets out to lay firm foundations for a lifetime as a teacher that will stretch into a future at best only dimly perceived, and be carried out in a thousand and one different situations. The student's experience in this formative period will go far towards shaping his or her attitudes and understandings; it should provide a body of knowledge and a range of skills that will meet immediate professional needs; and it should encourage an open mind and a desire to go on learning and developing. The initial training system cannot give the teacher everything he or she will need as the years unfold, nor can it be expected to. The teacher is only at the beginning of what should be a process of continual professional growth and renewal, with induction into the profession followed by a pattern of in-service training (INSET) across the years. The success of the initial training system must be measured by the quality of the foundation it lays, and by the thoroughness with which it prepares students for their professional responsibilities.

Those responsible for the initial training of teachers must keep a steady eye on those characteristics of effective teaching that appear to remain constant. They must be influenced, but undeterred, by the thoughts of changes that might or might not come, by the variations in children and their backgrounds, by the variety of schools their students will ultimately teach in, by the aspirations and values of parents, and by what, in the future, may be the intentions and aspirations for the education service of national and local politicians.

Every good teacher is first and foremost an individual, with particular strengths and weaknesses and personal quirks and enthusiasms that at one level defy generalisation. Nevertheless, it is possible to discern among the most effective teachers those characteristics of good teaching which can be generalised and which seem to persist over time, despite change and development. These characteristics, which are presented in *Education observed 3*[1], may seem no more than an ideal to which training should be directed, and yet it is one which some able students succeed in attaining by the final stages of their initial training. The characteristics revealed by inspection reports, like those identified in the national surveys of

---

[1]*Education observed 3: good teachers* DES, 1985. A paper by HMI

primary and secondary education[1], show that good teaching calls upon those aspects of personality and character which are needed to gain the respect of pupils. Among these are energy, enthusiasm, sensitivity, stamina, reliability, punctuality, a genuine interest in the young, a facility for communication, and a readiness to exercise the responsibility of caring for those in one's charge. Effective teachers help pupils develop lively, enquiring minds; acquire understanding, knowledge, and skills; develop personal moral values; and appreciate human achievement and aspirations. They have a sensitive understanding of the society in which their pupils are growing up, its racial and cultural mix, and the pace and effect of technological change. They are able to establish a quiet but purposeful working atmosphere, to organise the teaching and learning so that the work matches the different aptitudes and abilities of the children, and to relate and adapt their methods to the needs and circumstances of the moment. This entails setting high expectations, with pupils extended to their full capacity. To this end, the teachers employ class, group, and individual teaching to suit the kinds of learning demanded. The best teachers are well informed about individual pupils and are discerning in the identification of their needs. They use a variety of techniques to encourage and assess progress, including careful and informed observation, perceptive and constructive comment, and a variety of more formal measures. With such teachers the children attain high standards of work and are encouraged to live and work amicably together, to show consideration for others, and to have respect for their environment.

These characteristics are common in some measure to all good teachers and are constant and fundamental, but there are others which are specific to successful teaching of particular age-groups. Effective teachers in primary schools provide a broad curriculum which draws upon the personal experiences of the children, offering opportunities for well-focused teaching which deals with a subject in its own right and promotes learning in another, as for example where mathematics and language draw upon and in turn enrich the work in geography, history, and science. They provide younger children with opportunities for imaginative and constructive play and create situations within which the children can practise and master, as they grow older, the skills of observation and recording. They use a variety of teaching methods, and aim to nurture in the pupils the ability to develop and follow a line of argument, come to judgements, make discriminatory choices, develop skills and positive attitudes to learning and exercise leadership. In addition, those with special responsibilities for parts of the curriculum provide guidance and support for their colleagues by developing with them up-to-date schemes of work and by providing opportunities to discuss teaching methods, resources, and assessment practices. For this they need to have the time for reflection and planning in their leadership roles, and the ways in which they are deployed and supported will make increased demands upon the skills of management.

Many of the attributes of the good primary teacher are also needed by those who

---

[1] *Primary education in England* HMSO, 1978; *Aspects of secondary education in England* HMSO, 1979. Surveys by HMI

work with older pupils. Good secondary teachers seek to develop a style of classroom control which strikes a reasonable balance between the permissive and the authoritarian, where the pupils are praised wherever possible, where expectations are high, and where due regard is paid to attendance, punctuality, the completion of work, and consideration for other members of the group. In such a learning environment the confidence of the teacher and of the pupils is apparent, and the framework of sound relationships allows experimental methods to be tried and challenging tasks attempted.

Inspections of secondary schools have shown that good secondary teachers have command of their subject and are enthusiastic about teaching it, and perceive the contribution it can make to the whole curriculum. They use a range of resources and are not reliant on worksheets and the copying of notes. While they prepare their pupils well for public examinations they do not do so through the encouragement of narrowly-based cramming. They aim to develop a sense of enquiry, encourage speculative thinking, and involve the pupils in challenging investigations, but always on the basis of developing and understanding the essential facts and processes of the subject and a rigorous rejection of the slipshod and shoddy at any level.

Good secondary teachers are concerned to provide care of high quality for the pupils as individuals, understanding the close relationship which exists between academic and personal development, and to help them to make decisions, for example with reference to subject choices or possible careers. In preparing pupils for adult life, they keep in touch with further and higher education, industry, and developments in training. In this they have regard for the help which is available from other teachers, external agencies, and parents. They also come to know their pupils through sharing experiences both within and outside the school, through extra-curricular activities and through knowledge of the local community.

Those teachers who are heads of department, or in charge of subjects, should not only keep abreast of new developments in their fields but also provide guidance, supervision, and support to members of their teaching teams. They initiate and take part in regular discussion of current issues relating to policy and organisation, developing and putting into practice comprehensive schemes of work, and setting high expectations. And above all they are good models of teaching, displaying in themselves the personal qualities needed to bring out the best in colleagues and pupils.

New ways of organising the curriculum will need to be explored, for example in translating into practice the government's intention that, in years 4 and 5 in the secondary school, science shall be allocated a maximum of 20 per cent of total curriculum time and in introducing the Technical and Vocational Education Initiative (TVEI). Particular attention will also need to be given to the curriculum for pupils with special needs, to ensure that they have access to well balanced programmes which are integrated with the school curriculum as a whole, as far as this is possible, and are not confined to the use of a separate, alternative curriculum specific to them. To support and secure curricular changes, teachers are likely to be involved in designing and applying more refined and wider ranging assessment practices, encompassing, for example, practical, oral and aural skills, and personal qualities. They will continue to be involved in seeking to define with greater exactness the performances expected of children of differing ages, abilities, and aptitudes, and will have to be aware of the ways of identifying children with special educational needs and of the processes of identification introduced by the *Education Act 1981*. Important, too, will be an understanding of the value of assessment in improving pupils' performances.

The emphasis will need to be on providing pupils with the opportunities to show what they know and can do. In recording and reporting this, teachers, especially in secondary schools, will be involved much more generally than at present in developing pupil profiles and records of achievement. Teachers of older pupils will also be concerned with applying the general, subject, and grade-related criteria developed for the General Certificate of Secondary Education (GCSE), with assessment implications of the levels of achievement envisaged for the Certificate of Pre-Vocational Education (CPVE), and with the syllabuses for the Advanced Supplementary (AS) level examination. All teachers will need to be aware of the findings of the Assessment of Performance Unit (APU)[1] and to interpret and apply them in their teaching.

The qualities which are fundamental to good teaching will not change, whatever new demands are placed upon the teachers and the taught. Nevertheless, these demands will continue, as new ideas emerge and new policies evolve. They include those from government, for example as set out in its White Paper *Better schools*[2]; from the criteria for the GCSE; from the introduction of CPVE; from the messages coming out of specific initiatives such as TVEI; from specific grant related in-service initiatives; and from the social, economic and technological changes affecting society at large, employment, and education and training.

Initial training cannot prepare for all that a teacher may be called upon to do throughout a working lifetime. Nor can it be expected to turn out a finished product able to take a full part in the education service and meet all the demands of the day, let alone those that tomorrow will bring. Effective induction, positive support from more experienced colleagues, and continuing professional development all have their part to play in turning the beginner into a competent and experienced teacher able to ensure high standards of learning. Initial training must, however, turn out teachers who are enthusiastic about their subject interests and confident in their understanding of them; know about how children develop and learn; are able to relate to children and other adults; and can prepare, organise, and carry through their work and stand back to evaluate and review it. Above all, what has been achieved and mastered in initial training should enable new teachers to respond surely but flexibly, and with some imagination and flair, to their pupils in whatever particular teaching situation they find themselves.

---

[1] Details of APU's work and publications are available from APU, Room 4/77A, Elizabeth House, York Road, London SE1 7PH.

[2] *Better schools* Cmnd 9469. HMSO, 1985

Quality in schools: the initial training of teachers

This report considers in detail how well the initial training system was performing in meeting the demands which existed when the survey began, demands which have been well rehearsed in the early part of this Chapter. However, it seeks also to assess how well placed the system is to meet new and additional needs. To give a proper understanding of the scale of constraint and of the opportunities operating in the system it is necessary to outline briefly how it achieved its present nature. The following chapter describes changes in the system itself, in the context in which it functions, and in the demands made upon it. In conclusion, it sets out the survey's main findings.

2 The context of the survey, and its principal findings

The Context

The survey began in the early months of 1983, and at the end of a decade which had seen radical changes in the size and nature of the teacher training system. The most striking change had been the decline in the number of students in training, and in the number of institutions providing it. This process, which occurred throughout the four countries of the United Kingdom, reflected the fall in school rolls and the consequent reduced demand for teachers. In the early 1970s there were 180 public sector institutions and 27 universities providing teacher training in England and Wales, and between them they produced some 40,000 teachers each year. In 1977 plans were announced for the system to be modified to admit 20,000 students a year, the places to be provided by 84 public sector institutions and 27 universities. By 1982 further reductions were necessary, and the Secretary of State for Education in England directed that in the following year there would be only 15,650 admissions, though the proportion of students training for primary teaching was increased. By the beginning of the survey, the number of institutions in England continuing to provide initial teacher training had declined to 83; 56 in the public sector and 27 universities. Moreover, many of the former had changed in character. Ten years earlier almost all the public sector providers were monotechnic colleges of education, a few with 1500 or more on roll but many with student populations of between 300 and 700. The process of reduction has resulted not only in the closure of some colleges but also in the creation of a variety of new institutions. Some colleges of education have amalgamated with others, or with colleges of further education, to form larger units. Others have become part of polytechnics or, in a few cases, joined the school of education of a university. Few institutions now remain as monotechnics, most having introduced other vocational training and/or non-vocational degree courses.

In the course of the decade there had also been significant changes in the nature of the training. 89 per cent of the students leaving non-university institutions in 1972 had completed a three-year certificate course, for which there was no A-level requirement. Only a small minority remained for a fourth year and thus emerged with a Bachelor of Education (BEd) degree. After the committee chaired by Lord James of Rusholme produced its report[1] in 1972, the Government declared its

---

[1] *Teacher education and training.* Report of the Committee of Enquiry chaired by Lord James of Rusholme, HMSO, 1972.

intentions in a White Paper, *Education: a framework for expansion* HMSO, 1972. These included a policy for an all-graduate entry into the teaching profession, and over the following years there was a rapid growth in the number of BEd degrees, the final intake to almost all sub-degree certificate courses occurring in 1979. In that year, 88 per cent of the English institutions offered a three-year BEd unclassified degree with the opportunity of a four-year honours degree for suitable students. It is an indication of the rate of development that by 1985, when the survey was completed, 70 per cent of the institutions had phased out the unclassified degree and were recruiting for a four-year honours degree only.

The BEd degree[1] is the means by which most primary teachers now enter the profession, though one aspect of the substantial shift from secondary to primary training has been an increase also in the number admitted to the primary one-year postgraduate certificate course (PGCE) after completing a degree. In 1981 only 1500 were admitted to such courses; in 1984 the figure was 1850 (rising in 1985 to 2170). The PGCE has always been the principal route for entry to secondary teaching, and the 1982 reorganisation reduced further the contribution of the BEd to secondary school staffing. It was restricted thereafter to a relatively small number of secondary specialist subjects: physical education, home economics, craft, design and technology, business studies, mathematics, science, music, religious education, and drama. In the 1984 intake to English teacher training institutions these accounted together for only 34 per cent of all recruitment to public sector secondary training and 22 per cent of all secondary training, PGCE being the major source and the sole route into secondary teaching for all other subjects. The majority (61 per cent) of all secondary PGCE courses are provided by university departments of education. In some of the public sector institutions one effect of reduced commitment to secondary training during the period of the survey was to face members of staff with new and unaccustomed demands. Many had been recruited originally for their expertise in secondary teaching, and lacked the experience of primary schools which the institution now needed. Moreover, the reduction in the range of secondary subjects meant the loss of staff with subject expertise for some primary BEd courses. A number of the institutions in the survey were left without an adequate base in some important subjects of the school curriculum.

The decade up to 1983, when the survey began, saw an increase in the national attention directed towards the curriculum and organisation of schools, and the activity this generated inevitably had implications for the training of teachers. During the years 1976-1978, HMI carried out surveys of the organisation and work of primary and secondary schools in England, resulting in the publication of *Primary education in England* HMSO, 1978 and *Aspects of secondary education in England* HMSO, 1979. There followed, between 1982 and 1985, reports

---

[1] A small number of institutions offer Bachelor of Arts (BA) or Bachelor of Science (BSc) courses in which professional training for teaching can be taken alongside the study of the subject(s) or by means of an intercalated year, the total course lasting four years. None of these formed part of the survey.

on education from 5 to 9[1], and on 8 to 12[2] and 9 to 13[3] middle schools, and a study of Welsh schools resulted in *Curriculum and organisation of primary schools in Wales* HMSO, 1984. In Northern Ireland, the Inspectorate conducted during 1979-80 a survey of classroom practice in primary schools, and the Northern Ireland Council for Educational Development is in the course of publishing a series of guidelines on the primary curriculum. In 1982, the decision was taken to publish all HMI reports on individual schools in England and Wales, and since the appearance of the first in January 1983 there has been a steady flow of these. To date, reports have been issued on 279 primary schools and on 265 secondary schools. The published findings of these surveys and inspections have underlined the need for change and development in the training of teachers. For example, the HMI discussion paper *Teacher training and the secondary school* DES, 1981 looked at the evidence of the survey of English secondary schools and suggested that teacher training should focus increased attention on certain pressing needs in the teacher's repertoire: knowledge of his or her specialist subject; its relation to the rest of the curriculum and its bearing on the pupil's personal and social development; the ability to assess and establish appropriate levels of work; and an understanding of the needs of the less able. Evidence about the capacity of young teachers to meet the demands of the classroom was published in *The new teacher in school*[4]. Among a number of recommendations in the report, HMI suggested a more rigorous assessment of intending teachers during training, a better balance in the initial training courses, and a sound personal competence in the subject or area of the curriculum which the student had been trained to teach. The clearest implication of all was that teacher training must respond more directly to the needs of the schools and bring them into closer partnership in the professional preparation of teachers. HMI concerns about teacher training were mirrored by the findings of two research projects, funded by the DES and published in 1982.[5]

During the years in which HMI were carrying out their surveys of schools, they maintained their visits to teacher training institutions, inspecting work in progress, and assessing the extent to which developments were taking place. In addition, there were two specific surveys which resulted in published reports: *Developments in the BEd degree course* HMSO, 1979 and *PGCE in the public sector* DES, 1980. Their chief concern was the structure and balance of teacher training courses, and they reported on aspects of the undergraduate and postgraduate courses in 15 and 18 institutions respectively. Other, informal, surveys focused more closely on the work of students, both within the institutions and within schools, and upon the appropriateness of particular forms of training for the teachers they were aiming to produce. One survey took as its focus the preparation of teachers for the world of work, and this resulted in the publication of *Teacher training and preparation for*

---

[1] *Education 5 to 9: an illustrative survey of 80 first schools in England* HMSO, 1982.

[2] *Education 8 to 12 in combined and middle schools: a survey by HMI* HMSO, 1985.

[3] *9-13 middle schools: an illustrative survey* HMSO, 1983.

[4] *The new teacher in school* HMI Matters for Discussion No15. HMSO, 1982.

[5] McNamara, D R and Ross, A M *The BEd degree and its future* School of Education, University of Lancaster 1982; Patrick, H, Bernbaum, G, and Reid, K. *The structure and process of initial teacher education within universities in England and Wales,* School of Education, University of Leicester, 1982.

working life DES, 1982. From 1983 visits also took place to university departments of education, by invitation.

Throughout these and other visits there was extensive discussion with many people involved in the training of teachers. HMI took account of these discussions, and of the many articles and research projects on the subject, when preparing a discussion paper which drew principally upon the evidence of inspections in teacher training and of the inspections and surveys of schools. This paper was submitted in 1982 to the Advisory Committee on the Supply and Education of Teachers (ACSET) and to other bodies. It was considered by ACSET and HMI discussed it with validating bodies and professional associations. The outcome was a revised HMI discussion paper *Teaching in schools: the content of initial training* DES, 1983. ACSET had earlier submitted to the Secretaries of State its advice on the planning of teacher supply; it followed this with advice on the structure and content of initial training courses in England and Wales. The principal recommendation was that the Secretaries of State should establish criteria which they would take into account when deciding on the approval of courses of initial teacher training. The acceptance of this and other recommendations of ACSET formed part of the White Paper *Teaching quality* HMSO, 1983 and ACSET was asked to provide further advice on the criteria and on the machinery by which they might be applied to teacher education courses. As a result of ACSET's recommendations, the Secretaries of State decided to establish a Council for the Accreditation of Teacher Education (CATE) to advise them on the approval of initial teacher training courses in England and Wales. This was the subject of DES *Circular 3/84* and Welsh Office *Circular 21/84,* the annex to which set out in detail the criteria to be observed by CATE when preparing recommendations on the approval of individual initial teacher training courses.

Parallel developments were taking place in Northern Ireland. In January 1983, the Department of Education for Northern Ireland (DENI) issued a report entitled *Professional studies and professional development in teacher training in Northern Ireland.* The main recommendations were in harmony with those of the White Paper *Teaching quality* and called for greater emphasis on professional preparation, the involvement of schools in the assessment of students in training, and improved links between teacher training institutions and schools. Subsequently, DENI invited comment from interested parties on a proposal to associate Northern Ireland directly with CATE. The resulting decision to do so was announced in DENI *Circular 1985/20.*

In the context of the earlier interest in the training of teachers and of developments in the schools, it became clear that much would be gained from a substantial survey of initial training in England, Wales, and Northern Ireland.

Accordingly, a sample of 30 institutions was drawn, which represented 45 per cent of the public sector institutions in the three countries. Since the policy for teacher education in Scotland differs in many respects from that of the other three countries, Scottish institutions are not included in the survey report. However, a member of the Scottish Inspectorate was involved extensively in visits to the English institutions in the survey, and the discussions and exchange of information about developments in teacher education involved all four countries. The findings of this report relate, nevertheless, only to England, Wales, and Northern Ireland. Details of the design and planning of the survey are given in Appendix 1. The principal findings are given below, and Chapter 3 discusses a number of issues to which they give rise and which also take their origin in recent policy statements and developments noted in inspections and visits outside the scope of the survey.

The principal findings

Staffing and accommodation

Despite the recent history of contraction in teacher training, and the tight control of staff-student ratios, the number of staff was in all cases adequate for the demands of the initial training courses. The great majority of those contributing to the courses were judged to be well qualified academically, and almost all were qualified to teach in schools. Most had been in post for over a decade, and in the main their previous full-time teaching experience had been in secondary schools. Only a relatively small number had experience which was recent and appropriate for the increase in the training of primary teachers.

In the institutions where teacher training was offered alongside other undergraduate work, about half the BEd secondary specialist subject courses and a third of those offered to primary students were taught jointly with other degrees.

The management policies within institutions had a key role in determining the effectiveness of staff. Staff were on the whole deployed as effectively as possible in the light of the shortage of well-qualified and experienced primary specialists, and by the end of the survey period most institutions had made arrangements for some of those concerned with pedagogy to spend time teaching in schools, mostly on the basis of half a day or a day a week. There was scope, however, for more clearly formulated staff development policies which took account of the needs of the training course as a whole and of those of individual members of staff.

The organisation of work was at its most effective where staff worked cooperatively as a team with strong leadership and clearly defined responsibilities, which made best use of their talents and expertise.

Relationships between staff and students were almost uniformly excellent, and the level of pastoral care was generally good and often excellent.

In almost all the institutions, teacher training took place in purpose-built accommodation, and in the case of half of them this was on two or more sites. Much of the teaching accommodation was attractively located, but in a quarter of the institutions the accommodation showed serious deficiencies.

Few institutions carried out externally funded research, and in general the contribution of staff to research was small. There were, however, numerous excellent examples of individuals with good records of research and who had published successfully in fields directly related to their work. Many others were engaged in study for higher degrees.

Structure and content of primary training: BEd and PGCE courses

By the end of the survey, two-thirds of the BEd courses in the survey institutions offered only the four-year honours route. Most occupied 30 teaching weeks in each year, with class contact hours varying between 12 and 20 hours per week. The courses generally sought to prepare students as class teachers. All institutions provided compulsory curriculum courses in language and mathematics, varying in length, and the majority offered a range of relatively short compulsory curriculum courses covering the rest of the primary school curriculum. A few left out some areas, while others provided a compulsory core and options, with the effect that the range of the student's professional expertise was narrowed. It was evident that institutions found it difficult to meet satisfactorily the demands of both breadth and depth in curriculum courses within the current structure of their BEd, which allowed substantial time on educational and professional studies.

The time devoted to specialist subject study occupied on average 350 hours in three-year courses and 420 hours in four year courses but there was wide variation from one institution to another, with extremes of 135 hours and 600 hours. Most BEd primary students were able to choose their specialist study from at least six offered, and in some institutions from 12 or more. By the end of the survey, 85 per cent of those students whose courses offered a specialist subject were pursuing study broadly relevant to the primary curriculum. Nearly half were taking courses in the humanities, 17 per cent expressive arts, 10 per cent science − mainly biology, 7 per cent mathematics, 6 per cent social sciences, 4 per cent physical education and 3 per cent French (see Figure 1). In most instances the amount of time students spent on specialist study was insufficient to provide them with adequate knowledge and confidence in a particular area of the primary curriculum.

BEd subject studies for primary students were usually enjoyed by students and most of the sessions seen were satisfactorily or well taught. In general, the content of subject studies was similar to that found in other higher education courses and was not designed to relate directly to the primary curriculum. A small number of institutions offered subject studies which combined academic content with professional application, and some of these were of very good standard, illustrating the potential of this approach.

By the end of the survey, most institutions had moved towards a length of 36 weeks for their PGCE courses, with the number of class contact hours varying between 300 and 350 overall. This limited time span frequently caused difficulties for institutions in attempting to prepare students as class teachers and in giving them an adequate

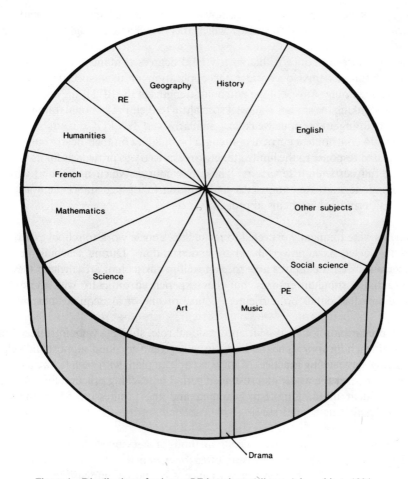

Figure 1   Distribution of primary BEd students (all years) by subject, 1984

range of professional skills. It was, however, evident that institutions had given much serious thought to means by which this disadvantage might be overcome.

It was a matter of concern that so few BEd degrees contained a method course designed for students to consider the application of their specialist subject to children's learning. As one of the potential strengths of the BEd is the opportunity it offers for linking the students' subject specialism to their professional training, this is a disappointing and serious weakness. Similarly, very few PGCE courses prepared students to contribute a curricular strength by building on their degree subjects. In general, the response to the limited time span was to try to provide as far as possible for the full curriculum repertoire. Those few courses which had found ways of exploiting the graduates' knowledge and enthusiasm for their subject demonstrated the wealth and value of this approach.

Students were frequently expected to relate their course work to school experience, and this acted as a powerful aid to understanding. During teaching practice, students showed themselves able to plan well in curriculum areas where they had substantial curriculum courses, but they experienced difficulty with those areas where they had either no curriculum course or one of inadequate substance.

In the preparation for their wider professional role, students were introduced to a range of teaching approaches and were usually given very good support and help in preparing for teaching practice. Many were able to plan, with such help, an outline of work to cover the whole of a sustained period of teaching practice, but they were less confident about long-term planning and the progressive development of knowledge, concepts, and skills.

All students were at least introduced to methods of assessing children's attainments and progress, but the coverage was often brief and the diagnostic value of the informed analysis of children's performance was seldom emphasised sufficiently.

Students met with varying degrees of success in attempting to cater for the full range of individual differences found in ordinary primary school classes. Although initial training can do no more than lay a foundation for students' understanding and diagnosing of learning differences in individual pupils, the weakness in this aspect of professional competence gave cause for concern.

At the time of the survey many courses were being restructured to take account of the wider conception of special educational needs set out in the Warnock Report[1] and in the *Education Act 1981*. Approaches in BEd ranged from distinct units on special needs to models where the topic was intended to permeate work in most parts of the course. About three quarters of the institutions were proving successful in putting their strategies into practice. In the remainder, and notably those where the work was not directly applied in schools, the courses on special needs gave cause for concern.

---

[1] *Special educational needs.* Report of the Committee of Enquiry chaired by Mrs H M (now Lady) Warnock. HMSO, 1978.

About a third of the institutions gave considerable time and emphasis to preparing students for work in a multi-ethnic society, and a substantial number were reviewing their policies in this area and adjusting their course content, although a minority gave it insufficient attention. There were numerous individual examples of good practice.

Most institutions gave some attention to home-school relationships and some good work was seen. There was considerable variation in the extent to which students were given the opportunity for acquiring a thorough understanding of the topic, and those training to teach early years classes were most likely to be successful in this.

Students were acquiring a good grasp of techniques of class control. Practically all those observed on teaching practice had established good relationships with the children and few experienced serious difficulties of control.

A quarter of the institutions offered a BEd primary course which included a nursery component, but only a minority of these provided adequate training for nursery teachers. With few exceptions, in courses which encompassed the 3 to 8 age range the emphasis was on the 5 to 8 role. The lack of staff expertise in the early years, and the consequent emphasis on approaches appropriate for older children, is a cause for concern.

Structure and content of secondary training: BEd and PGCE courses

The provision of secondary BEd courses, now confined to a relatively small number of subjects, generally included at least two years of study of the students' main and subsidiary specialist teaching subjects. Because of recruitment difficulties in some shortage areas, institutions had increased their intake to other subjects, notably physical education (PE). In the BEd courses in the survey 40 per cent of the students were taking PE, 20 per cent home economics, 8 per cent craft, design and technology, 7 per cent mathematics, 6 per cent religious education, 6 per cent science, and fewer than 2 per cent music (see Figure 2 overleaf).

The majority of students in the subject method courses in BEd and PGCE were gaining a good grasp of the approaches and methods appropriate to the successful teaching of their subject. In a substantial number of cases the preparation for this role was particularly commendable. There were, however, a few courses where the specialist preparation had serious deficiencies.

In the majority of BEd courses some constructive links were being drawn between specialist subject studies and the corresponding method courses. There was less evidence, both in BEd and PGCE courses, of links between subject method courses and education studies.

In general, the BEd and PGCE courses did not give any substantial attention to the relationship between individual subjects and the whole curriculum, and some did not address the issue at all.

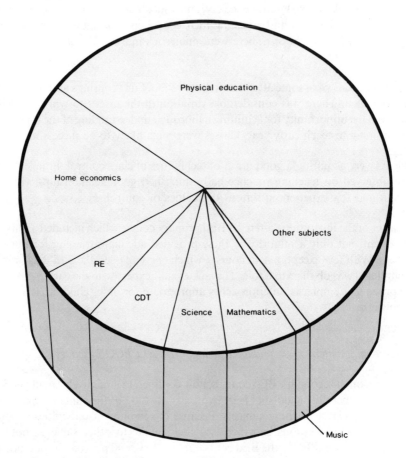

Figure 2 Distribution of secondary BEd students (all years) by subject, 1984

In the majority of the lessons observed on teaching practice, students had established good relations with pupils and were controlling classes well. In some of the exceptions, inexperienced students had been given classes which presented difficulties even to experienced teachers.

Only about half the subject method courses in either BEd or PGCE were providing students with an understanding of the variety of individual pupils' needs or helping them to make the teaching of their subject relevant to the full range of pupils they would meet. This was an area of professional training which gave cause for concern.

The most prevalent form of provision for special educational needs was a short common course supplemented by options. A small number of institutions had adopted with varying success the approach of giving responsibility for treatment of the topic to individual tutors in various parts of the course (the 'permeation' approach). A few institutions made no provision at all other than through optional courses.

There were some outstandingly good examples of attention to differences in the ethnic background of pupils, but this aspect of initial training was generally not well developed in secondary courses.

Students were acquiring a particularly good understanding of their role in relation to the pupils' personal and social development where there was collaboration between subject method and education studies courses.

Only about half the institutions were dealing effectively with the assessment of pupils' progress. An even smaller proportion of courses provided an adequate introduction to the public examination system.

In a small number of institutions there was some imaginative coverage of the world of work and the industrial and commercial relevance of the school curriculum, but in general this aspect was not well developed.

Relationships with schools

On average, BEd students spent about a sixth of their courses in schools, mainly in the form of block practice or serial visiting, and the experience was for the most part well structured. The proportion for PGCE students was almost half of the course time. Serial attachment, notably where tutor, class teacher, and students worked together in the classroom, emerged as a particularly valuable aspect of training.

A less satisfactory aspect of school experience in some institutions was provision for the fourth year of the BEd course. Many students had insufficient practical experience during this crucial stage of their training.

During their time in schools, the majority of students worked with teachers who provided support and guidance. There were, however, too many cases where students were exposed to poor practice.

There was a clear advantage where a mutual understanding existed between training institutions and schools on the matter of aims and methods of teaching. Tutors particularly valued long-standing contacts with local schools, though there was some evidence of schools being used out of habit, with insufficient attention to their change in character.

Careful attention was given to providing students with a variety of experience, in relation to the differing ages and abilities of pupils, their social background, and the type of school they attend. However, the students' experience of good quality teaching was less common, and some were restricted by narrow and outdated practice in schools to which they were allocated for their teaching practice.

The involvement of local education authorities in the selection of schools for teaching practice was not widespread, and there is scope for more extensive consultation with LEA advisers. In those few cases where advisers were involved, the results were particularly valuable.

The head, or commonly in secondary schools a senior teacher, played an important part in determining which class and teacher would be offered to work with the student. Some exercised careful judgement in reaching their decision, but there were numerous instances of students being inappropriately placed within the school.

Most institutions provided schools with documents about individual students and the courses they were following. These documents varied greatly both in scope and quality, but most schools felt that they were satisfactorily served in this respect.

The nature and thoroughness of preparation for teaching practice varied between and within institutions, and there was some work of high quality. In the best examples, the schools received preliminary visits from tutors, and the teachers were well informed about the students' degree backgrounds, the nature of their courses, their personalities, professional strengths and weaknesses, and areas where further experience would be valuable.

There was also considerable variation in the quality of the students' preparation of schemes of work and of plans for individual lessons. The most important shortcoming was lack of precision and a failure to identify objectives for what the pupils would learn.

There was little evidence of any specific training for those teachers designated as responsible within the school for students on teaching practice. There is scope for the development of structures, support, and in-service training, designed to improve the supervision of students in schools.

It was exceptional for schools to share the responsibility for the assessment of students' practical teaching. Class teachers were particularly uncertain of their role in this respect, and this is an aspect of partnership which warrants closer attention and improvement.

For a variety of reasons, which included restrictions on time and resources, the extent and nature of the supervision of students by college tutors during block practice gave rise to concern.

Institutions were increasingly encouraging serving teachers to contribute to initial training, both through participation in the teaching of courses and through representation on college committees. In some cases the teachers were formally designated as teacher-tutors and recognised as such by their local authorities. Contributions from teachers should be considered by all institutions for inclusion in their policies for relations with schools.

The students and their work

Institutions took considerable pains in the selection and interviewing of applicants for places on BEd and PGCE courses, and there was evidence of the growing involvment of practising teachers in the process. There were a number of cases, notably in secondary PGCE, where the selection process was particularly impressive.

In the selection of primary students, the majority of the PGCE candidates accepted had degrees which related closely to aspects of the primary curriculum. Though there were some instances of degrees which could not be considered appropriate, there was a good match between the degree qualifications of PGCE secondary students and the courses for which they were enrolled.

In the majority of cases the criteria for selecting candidates to study the main subjects within BEd were adequate. There was, however, evidence that the field from which to select was limited in some of the secondary shortage subject courses and that some students enrolled for those subjects lacked the necessary background to tackle the demands of the course. Of the BEd students admitted on the basis of GCE, about a third had three passess at A-level and a half had two; a typical profile was two passes, one at Grade C and one at Grade D, which represents an A-level points score of five.

Overall, the written work produced by students was competent and in a number of instances exhibited high quality. The level of oral work was generally satisfactory, though not all students were being provided with sufficient opportunity to participate freely in discussion. In practical work in secondary courses, including science, mathematics, and drama, the work was reasonably competent and in some instances reached a high standard.

The majority of the students observed at work in schools were teaching satisfactorily. Among their principal strengths were the quality of the relationships they developed with pupils and the time and thought given to the preparation of lessons. Where weaknessess occurred, the most common were: failure to identify clear teaching objectives; a tendency to identify planning with simply listing tasks or assembling materials; failure to identify the individual learning differences between pupils; and a lack of match between content and/or method and the needs of a mixed ability group of pupils.

3   Issues arising from the survey

General

In the opening paragraph of this report it was emphatically affirmed that the education and training of the teacher should be seen as a continuous process. The key importance of the initial training stage is to lay a foundation for this process and to equip the emerging teacher with the capacity to meet his or her professional responsibilities and to continue to grow and develop. The demands which teaching makes upon those who practise it grow ever more complex, and Government policies have classified and ordered these within the framework of a set of aims to improve the quality of learning and teaching in our schools. The report seeks to indicate the extent of success with which teacher training institutions have performed their existing role, and gives pointers to their potential to meet the new challenges with which developments have faced them. This Chapter examines a number of those key issues and assesses the response that will need to be made by the initial training institutions and by the profession at large.

The implications of the findings of the survey are that this response should be radical. Developments during the survey and those noted in more recent inspections and visits show that many institutions have recognised that it will involve a reappraisal of the courses as a whole, since what is needed cannot be achieved by addition and minor modification. For the local authorities and the schools it will mean an extension of their role in the initial training of teachers, and of the part they play in the teachers' continued professional development, from induction onwards. There are already signs of much positive activity. In response to the criteria set out in DES *Circular 3/84,* many institutions have radically changed the structure of their courses, and others are in the process of doing so. They have also considered carefully the capacity of lecturers to teach the new courses, have recruited new lecturers, and have drawn the schools into closer partnership. Many schools, for their part, have responded well and have recognised that practising teachers are key figures in preparing others to enter their profession. There remains, nevertheless, a great deal to be done. The sections that follow examine the extent of this and the implications for action on the part of all concerned.

Relations with schools

The notion of a partnership between teacher training institutions and schools has come to be recognised as one of great importance. It enables the various elements of the teacher training course to be closely linked with practical experience. Practising teachers become actively involved in the process, sharing responsibility for the planning, supervision, and assessment of the students' school-based work and also taking part in the training of the students within the institutions. The partnership also benefits schools themselves, since the experience and knowledge of colleagues from the teacher training institutions become available as a valuable source of support. There is no doubt that institutions have given increased attention to their relations with schools. There has been a growth in the participation of practising teachers in the selection of applicants for admission to teacher training. There has also been a growth in the involvement of teachers in the teaching of the initial training course, and in the activities of tutors within schools. This activity reflects great credit on all concerned, and it is encouraging to find that so many of those involved are giving thought to further steps they might take. Some of these might be worth closer consideration here.

The extended participation of teachers in the selection of initial training students needs careful consideration, in terms both of its nature and of the implications for resources. At present it chiefly takes the form of the participation of the teacher in the interviewing of candidates. This undoubtedly has value, but there is scope for the development of other ways of bringing to bear the insights of practising teachers upon the selection process. For example, one institution has arranged for applicants to spend part of a day in a school and has invited members of the teaching staff to offer their views on the candidates' suitability, based on observation of the way they relate to children, the questions they ask, the interest and enterprise they show, etc. Initiatives of this kind present logistical difficulties, but they appear to provide particularly valuable information. The whole field of teachers' involvement in the selection process is one which calls for further thought and experimentation, but whatever form it takes there are clear implications for reviewing the teaching resources of the school. At present, development is to some extent hampered by the difficulties arising from the replacement of teachers who are released to assist with selection, and this will need to be recognised by LEAs in reviewing the deployment of their teaching force.

Similar considerations apply to the involvement of school teachers in the teaching of the courses within institutions. There is encouraging evidence that this is a growing practice, and institutions and schools have been enterprising in developing a variety of means of providing for it. Among these have been joint appointments, teacher-tutor exchange, and regular or occasional lectures or tutorial work. If such activity is to be expanded, institutions will have to organise it carefully within the framework of their policy for relations with schools. Teachers sometimes need support in adjusting to the needs of adult learners, and there is likely to be a call upon additional resources if an extension of teacher release is involved.

The principal focus of the partnership between teachers and teacher trainers will always be the schools themselves. Where and in what circumstances the students gain their practical experience is of the highest importance. The report indicates that it was not uncommon for students to be exposed to poor models of teaching in schools, and in some cases for them to be required to conform to practice which was at odds with the methods advocated on their course. In such circumstances, students should be helped to recognise good and bad practice and develop confidence in holding to the principles which underpin the former. Some tutors in secondary subject method courses have developed a close relationship with a small number of subject departments within schools. Often they teach in the department themselves, perhaps for a day a week or when the students are at the school for serial experience. Similarly, primary tutors have formed close associations with particular primary schools, or classes within those schools. One example of this kind of activity, IT-INSET[1] (Initial Training-In-Service Training) where teacher, tutor, and students are working together with shared goals, is potentially an excellent means of providng school experience but requires careful preparation and detailed planning. At the other end of the scale is the allocation of two or three students to a school on no other basis than that the school is prepared to accept that number. As the amount of time spent in schools increases it becomes a matter of importance that students be placed in the best possible schools and with the best practitioners within them. One implication of this is the notion of the 'associated school', selected on the basis of a detailed knowledge of its qualities resulting from a close working partnership.

Whatever form the selection of schools takes, there is a strong case for greater involvement of the LEA, and of advisers in particular. It is, moreover, impossible to emphasise too strongly the value of tutors themselves teaching within the schools. This not only enhances their credibility with the school staff, but is second to none as a means of getting to know the schools thoroughly for the purpose of placing students. The tutors need to know the school well to develop a sympathetic understanding of its aspirations, and to support the student appropriately. The school teachers, conversely, need to understand the objectives of the college course, and the specific objectives of any part of the school experience. The range of what the school offers could be extended greatly beyond what is commonly found. For example, students might be invited into curriculum planning meetings, or provided with collections of work to illustrate varieties of performance, particularly to lift their expectations of what children are capable of. Teacher, tutor, and student alike should work together in planning school experience at its various stages. All concerned should always be quite clear about what they are aiming to do during school experience. As this experience cumulatively takes effect the students' capacity for self-evaluation should be developed, and this is something to which institutions should give more thought. It is evident from the survey that many teachers are still uncertain of their role in

---

[1]A pattern of working developed by a research project funded by the DES; students, tutors, and teachers work together cooperatively in the school classroom, to the professional benefit of each.

the training process, or of the value placed upon the assessment they make of the student's performance. There is a task here for institutions and for the heads of the schools themselves. The best kind of practice is based on first-class documentation, thorough briefing, regular meetings between teachers and tutors, and active involvement of the latter in the life of the school. Teachers must be enabled to see that they have a recognised and important role in the supervision and assessment of the student and in the process of relating theory and practice.

The supervision of students while on teaching practice emerged as one of the more worrying aspects of the survey's findings. In the first place there was the question of the frequency and duration of visits by tutors, and in the second there was that of specialist support. There is no doubt that tutors have many demands upon them, and the extent to which they are able to visit students is often limited by institutional pressures of time and of financial constraints. Providing a sound programme of supervision is a matter for institutional policy, the first consideration of which should be the support and assessment of the student. This suggests that students should be able to count on regular and substantial visits by specialist tutors, who are able to relate the progress and needs of the student to what is being provided − or needs to be provided − in the course. The survey revealed that while most students were able to plan and conduct an individual lesson competently, they were less successful in long-term planning and in their attention to the progressive development of pupils' knowledge, concepts, and skills. Some also had difficulty in effectively evaluating their own teaching. While undoubtedly these are aspects of professional competence which only time and experience will develop fully, the process should be founded during initial training. They need the explicit attention of the supervising tutor and teacher. Equally, the assessment of the student's performance should be applied not only to his or her immediate needs but to indications of continuing professional needs at the induction stage and later. There is clearly scope for the development of in-service provision for supervising tutors and for their counterparts in the schools, and for the extensive exchange between institutions of information about good practice.

The content of undergraduate courses for intending primary teachers

The range and depth of knowledge needed by the teacher in the primary school is considerable, and it has to be able to answer to complex demands. *Better schools*[1] (paragraph 62) sums these up well: 'teaching the broad curriculum outlined in paragraph 61, and doing so with the necessary differentiation, places formidable demands on the class teacher which increase with the age of pupils. Older primary pupils (including those in middle schools) need to benefit from more expertise than a single class teacher can reasonably be expected to possess; this has consequences for staffing and the deployment of staff within a school, including the use of teachers as consultants'. Statements such as these, and the views of the schools themselves, point to the centrality of curriculum studies in the training process. It is essential for

---

[1]Cmnd 9469. HMSO, 1985.

primary teachers to acquire both an effective grasp of a broad curriculum repertoire, and a deeper knowledge of some specialised aspect of it. This can be achieved only if the institution makes available adequate resources in terms of time and staffing strength. Some institutions are attaining this with considerable success. Their courses, both BEd and PGCE, are designed in such a way as to achieve coherence, with wider professional and educational issues studied within the context of curriculum study, and all of these tried against classroom conditions in school experience and teaching practice. They have appointed lecturers with recent successful experience of primary school teaching, extended the practical experience of existing lecturers, and drawn upon teachers in the schools. Many other institutions have a good deal to do before their curriculum courses are on the way to achieving a balance of breadth and depth. As they at present stand it is unlikely that students would acquire a confident grasp of the elements of a broad curriculum, and still less likely that they would acquire special expertise in a particular part of that curriculum. Chapter 5 makes clear how in BEd, and even more acutely in PGCE, very small amounts of time were sometimes allocated to important areas of the primary school curriculum. Course design is a complex undertaking, but it is difficult to understand, for example, how in a four year course religious education can be allocated as little as 1 per cent of the available time and mathematics less than 4 per cent.

During the course of the survey DES *Circular 3/84* emerged, with its clear requirements of at least two years of subject study for every intending teacher, at a level appropriate to higher education. In the case of primary teachers this could possibly mean the equivalent of 1.5 years studying the subject or curricular area in its own right and one half-year on its application to the learning needs of primary school children. The evidence of the survey suggests that the BEd courses in most institutions fell considerably short of providing adequate subject study, and that scarcely any had developed aspects of the course which would equip students to orient that study to the needs of primary school children. Already, however, most institutions are revising and reconstructing their courses to meet this criterion. They are doing so in a variety of ways, many of them providing the specialist study in the form of a single subject, often jointly taught with BA or BSc students, some seeking to conceive it in terms of a grouping of two or more related subjects. Specialist subject study on this scale will pose a new challenge to most institutions. Some single subject courses may offer units which are particularly appropriate to work in a primary school and which students may take in addition to their core studies. Others may be undifferentiated from the material being studied by BA or BSc students. It is likely in such cases that the content of the subject study will not have been selected for its specific relevance to the teacher's professional needs. If these are to be met, then the work in curriculum studies which takes up the professional application of the subject will need to be particularly carefully devised and staffed. Equally challenging will be the designing of courses where specialist subject study is conceived in terms of a wider area of the curriculum. A grouping of humanities, for example, or of expressive arts, will need to be guaranteed teaching at an appropriate academic level, particularly where the constituent parts remain discrete and each has a time allocation of little more than half a year.

In devising and teaching methodological courses related to the student's specialist subject study most institutions will be breaking completely new ground. The general practice currently is for students to take a curriculum course common to all, whatever their specialist subject, and these courses seldom offer differentiated work matched to the individual knowledge and experience of the students. This aspect of the student's professional training will face institutions with a number of challenges which have implications for management, staffing, and relations with schools. Viability of group size will be an issue. Where possible, each subject should have its own group for the study of its application, but where numbers are small it may be necessary to group two or three closely related subjects for a course which identifies common teaching approaches. The deployment of lecturers will be another key factor. Such courses will need the combined knowledge and skills of specialists in the subject, or area of the curriculum, and tutors with an expert understanding of primary school methods and approaches. Cooperative working and clear leadership will be essential. The courses themselves will need to consider the interpretation of the subject and its orientation to the primary classroom, and will need to relate to them the important professional issues, such as individual learning differences, assessment, and classroom organisation. The primary PGCE course poses particular problems, but equally offers stimulating opportunities. The students may bring with them knowledge in depth of one or more particular subjects from their undergraduate studies, but the pressures of time make it difficult for institutions to provide specifically for the application of this knowledge to the needs of primary school children. The time for curriculum study in general is more restricted than in BEd, and if the demands of breadth and depth are to be met as far as is possible then course design and the deployment of staff will need to be a management priority.

An important agent in the development of all primary students' specialist abilities will be the schools themselves. The deployment of consultant strength in primary schools is not at present a widespread practice, and not all students have access to experience of such ways of working. They will need to be provided with more extensive opportunities to see such organisational patterns in practice, to recognise their potential, and to participate in them themselves. There is obviously scope for a great deal of development in this area, in which the active involvement of LEA advisers will be significant. In the college-based part of the course, students should become accustomed to sharing their specialist strengths, recognising what they have to offer and what others have to offer them, and above all coming to regard cooperative working as an essential professional skill.

Throughout the Chapters on training for primary teaching in Part II there are references to the pressures upon time and the under-representation of certain aspects of professional preparation. There seems no doubt that these pressures will continue to be felt in PGCE, even in the extended form it is taking in response to DES *Circular 3/84*. The extension to 36 weeks will expand the opportunities, but it will remain difficult in so limited a period of time to provide for all that a primary teacher needs to learn. The evidence of the survey suggests that primary courses are attracting able graduates, and the PGCE route will depend to a large extent for its success upon their capacity to assimilate and apply the wide range of knowledge and skills which have to be acquired in a relatively short period of time. It will be a priority for institutions to deploy the time effectively. It will also be important to ensure that all graduates recruited to PGCE have degrees which relate closely to the primary school curriculum. Even if these conditions are met, there will remain a need for a carefully structured programme of induction in the first year of teaching. The same measure of priority will be demanded in the disposition of time in the BEd course, but here the difficulties should be much less acute. It is immediately clear that the three-year BEd is faced with all the problems of the PGCE without its attendant starting strengths, and such degrees, steadily diminishing in number, must be regarded as at a serious disadvantage. Within a four year BEd it should be possible to organise the time in such a way that the various needs are fulfilled, and certainly possible to avoid some of the inadequate time allocations observed in the course of the survey once priorities are identified.

The report focuses at various points upon certain aspects of professional competence with which teachers in training need more help. Foremost among these are the ability to assess the performance of pupils and their potential development, and teach to that assessment; provide for a wide diversity of pupils' needs within any given class; and plan for the progressive growth of pupils' knowledge, concepts, and skills. The development of such competencies on the part of the teacher is a process which takes time and experience. If teachers are to be able to make judgements about pupils' performance, and identify features of their development, then they need the accumulating experience of work at various levels of achievement. Similarly, the long-term planning of pupils' knowledge and skills can be properly monitored only when its effects can be observed over a period of time. Nevertheless, it is essential for all teachers in training to recognise the importance of these professional competencies and to acquire an understanding of the ways in which they can be most effectively applied. The assessment of performance, for example, in any given subject requires a knowledge of that subject and the progressive demands it makes upon a pupil. This the student has to learn, and the application of it throughout successive school experiences and teaching practices will lay down the foundation for continued development in service.

Professional issues

The ability to work cooperatively and effectively as a team is an attribute teachers of all phases will need to possess in growing measure. The report points to a great divergence in practice across a range of developing professional issues which will be of increasing importance in training for primary and secondary schools: special educational needs, in the light of the 1981 Act; assessment of pupils' progress; individual learning differences; multi-ethnic education; relations with parents and the community; information technology; a perspective on aspects of the adult world beyond school; and economic awareness. These are issues which invite careful planning by all institutions, since they present a challenge not only in terms of the knowledge and experience the students will need, but of staff expertise and of the forms of organisation best calculated to provide them. The report shows that key issues such as these are too often offered as options which many students may not take. There are also disadvantages in discrete compulsory units, which are often too short to allow a full exploration of the complexities of the issues and are isolated from the rest of the course. Consideration of these and other such issues needs to reach into all the components of the course. They will take on the greatest significance for the specialist secondary teacher, for example, when they are seen as an essential dimension of the teaching and learning of the subject. Similarly, the primary teacher will see them as needing to inform all the activities of the classroom throughout the curriculum. This points to the need for an understanding of these issues to be acquired in context, which in turn suggests what has come to be known as the 'permeation' approach. The operation of such a way of working poses considerable organisational problems. It presupposes efficient coordination and cooperative working, with built-in expert support for those tutors responsible for curriculum work and subject methodology. Every institution should have tutors with designated responsibility for the specific issues listed above. It should be their role not only to teach such core units as are felt to be necessary but to coordinate all the work upon them in appropriate contexts in the course. Such tutors would therefore need to work closely with all others involved in the training process, for example the specialist phase tutors teaching the early years course or the specialist subject tutors responsible for secondary science method, providing material and guidance on how it could best be mediated. These are again matters for management at the appropriate level to consider closely, and they have implications for the development of planned policies and for the deployment of teaching and other resources.

The attainment of desirable professional standards at the end of a training course must depend to a large extent on the personal and intellectual qualities of the students recruited. It was reassuring to find that institutions employ careful procedures for recruitment, but any course of professional training is dependent at least in some measure, for the quality of the students it acquires, on the perceived attraction of the job for which it prepares. In the case of teaching, students who apply for the BEd course are making a positive choice of that profession, often at a relatively early age, and their perception of teaching includes relationships with pupils and colleagues, conditions of service, public esteem and financial reward. The combination of these factors in the motivation of applicants is still such as to provide each year substantial numbers of well qualified and well fitted entrants to BEd courses, but the undergraduate route into teaching has not been free from recruitment difficulties. During the period of the survey, the 18-plus population was at a record high level and applications to undergraduate courses were generally buoyant. Previous years had, however, seen severe under-recruitment to BEd courses, and recent figures for 1985 and 1986 do not give cause for confidence: in future years numbers of 18 year olds will decline, while the demands of industry and commerce for good graduates will increase.

Equally, although some candidates with good A-level scores continue to present themselves, the overall average A-level score for BEd entrants in the public sector of higher education is not high. This has particular implications for the way in which teaching and learning must be organised if the final academic and professional performance is to be as high as the demands of the profession imply.

The PGCE has sustained a very satisfactory level of recruitment, both in overall numbers and as measured by class of degree on entry. The commitment and motivation of the overwhelming majority of students on both BEd and PGCE courses were a credit to the selection process and to student-staff relationships, as well as to the young people themselves.

Management

Initial training is a complex and demanding process. The courses through which it is provided must bring together a range of widely divergent elements, often involving large numbers of staff and several departments. These elements have to be fused into a cohesive offering to students, in a manner which ensures that they acquire the knowledge and professional skills that good teaching requires. This presents a demand for good management which, in the institutions visited, had not always been met. For example, in some institutions only a small proportion of staff concerned mainly with BA and BSc degree work contributed to BEd courses, which suggests that a potentially valuable contribution to initial training was remaining largely untapped. Another difficulty that had not always been successfully tackled was the coordination of the work of large numbers of staff, many of whom made only minor contributions to the course. All the evidence indicates that the most effective courses were those with strong leadership which established clear goals and offered practical solutions to difficult problems.

If the teacher training system is to respond effectively to the challenges facing it, every institution will need as a priority a strong policy for staff development, carefully related to staff deployment. The most urgent need at the present time is to bring up to date the experience of staff in teaching in schools the age-group for which they are training students. The lack of recent teaching experience in primary schools among many tutors on primary courses is a matter for pressing attention. A feature of the lecturers' development policy will be the appointment of coordinators, knowledgeable in themselves, and capable of offering leadership to others, in certain fields: special educational needs; technological developments; education in inner cities; economic awareness; the applied curriculum; and multi-ethnic issues. Few institutions currently have such identifiable strength across all these fields, and arrangements for appropriate training and experience for specific individuals should be developed as quickly as possible.

Similarly, a responsibility of management in the evolution of partnership must be to ensure that good relationships are developed with the local authorities and their advisory teams, as well as with individual schools. These relationships should also form the framework in which the policies for updating tutors in their own school teaching experience are put into practice. The involvement of tutors in teaching in schools can be and should be undertaken in a way which is of visible benefit to the schools, and is valued as such by the teachers with whom they are working. The initiatives of individual lecturers are not sufficient to ensure the complex relationships which will be of abiding benefit to the pre-service and in-service needs of the teaching profession. Those who manage institutions and departments concerned with the training of teachers must accept the overall responsibility for the structuring of close and effective relationships with their partners in the education service.

Continuing professional development

The extension of partnership with schools will bring into clearer perspective the relationship between the initial and continuing education and training of teachers. Lack of understanding has sometimes led schools to a critical view of initial training because it sends them teachers who still need a great deal of help and guidance. The notion of 'extended professionalism' is not a new one, but it is one that has not been fully and universally recognised. The expectations should be laid down during initial training, and the process should begin with induction. A survey[1] into LEAs' provision for induction and in-service training showed how uncertain are the opportunities for a newly qualified teacher to continue to develop his or her knowledge and skills. *The new teacher in school* HMSO, 1982 underlined how important it is that they be able to do so. There is a clear indication that the individual needs of the young teacher should be identified, and that the induction process should be designed to meet them. The training institution, the school, and the local authority are partners in this process.

In September 1984, the Advisory Council for the Supply and Education of Teachers (ACSET) submitted to the Secretaries of State a report recommending major changes in the arrangements for planning and funding in-service education and training. The Government's response is recorded in *Better schools* (paragraphs 172-176) where it endorsed the case for 'a much more systematic approach .... to the planning of in-service training at school and LEA level, which would seek to match training both to the career needs of the teachers and to desired curricular changes in schools'. The new specific grants scheme, which came into operation on 1 April 1987, has a potentially significant contribution to make to the continuing professional development of the teaching force. But no less important will be a continual personal and collective commitment on the part of the teachers themselves to such development, and a readiness to see their career as one of continuing growth.

The foundations for this view of professional life must be established during initial training. Students should become accustomed to question, to debate, to analyse, to argue from evidence, and to examine their own habitual assumptions. They should accept that self-evaluation, and appraisal by others, are essential to the conduct of professional life.

---

[1] Survey of local authority arrangements for induction and in-service training of teachers (the INIST survey), conducted by the DES, 1982-83.

The response of the initial training system to new developments gives some promise for the future. It is evidence of its readiness to adapt to new demands if these are made clear and explicit. The challenge of Government policies for the curriculum, for examinations, and for access to good teaching for all children calls for a well educated and professionally skilled teaching force. Those who train this force deserve clear guidance, adequate help and resources, and an institutional structure which provides a suitable climate for the development of academic and professional excellence. In achieving its objectives the teacher training system will need the partnership of the teaching profession, other contributors to the higher education system, and both national and local Government, as well as the support of the broader community who share the concern for improvement in the nation's schools.

Quality in schools: The initial training of teachers

PART II
Detailed picture

4 The institutions

Staffing

Total staffing

Staffing structures in the survey's initial teacher training institutions have developed within the context of recent national developments in higher education generally. Firstly, all the survey institutions have been influenced profoundly by the rapid reduction in initial teacher training places referred to in Chapter 2. More than two thirds of the institutions were in fact the outcomes of amalgamations of institutions which had taken place as a result of these reductions. Secondly, in recent years there has been increasing pressure on resources for higher education at large, leading to a re-definition of the staff : student ratio (SSR). Although some new appointments were made, numbers of teaching staff continued to diminish in many institutions over the period of the survey, as adjustments became necessary.

Despite these changes, in none of the survey institutions was the quantity of staffing at the end of the survey judged to be insufficient to meet the initial teacher training needs of the students enrolled. However, the match between qualifications and duties was not uniformly close. Reductions in staffing had in many instances been governed by criteria other than that of suitability for the tasks in hand. Some staff, for example, had volunterred for early retirement on personal grounds. Some, within diversified colleges and polytechnics, were able by virtue of their subject expertise to transfer to teach on courses other than those involving teacher education. Within each establishment the result was that some aspects of the work were generously staffed, some understaffed, and some staffed by people whose qualifications and experience were inappropriate to the work they were being expected to undertake. In the polytechnics, teacher training was seen as one small part of a whole range of advanced further education (AFE) activities some of which were facing staff reductions. Within their context, the initial training courses were moving swiftly towards the SSR of 1 to 12 being advocated by the National Advisory Body (NAB).

In some institutions, problems arose where main subjects had been dropped, eg in BA or in secondary level BEd courses. Staff had departed and the institutions' primary courses were then left short of expertise in those subject areas. The subjects most affected tended to be those in which the specialist teams had been fairly small in the first place; music, art, and religious education were notable casualties. In one polytechnic, for example, the termination of a BA religious studies course had been accompanied by the retirement of the head of department and the resignations of two departmental staff, leaving only one religious studies specialist to handle all the PGCE and BEd work in this area.

In those institutions offering BA or BSc degrees, some at least of the staff concerned primarily with initial training also contributed to these courses. This kind of involvement was more extensive in colleges which provided such diversified degrees than in the polytechnics in the survey. In the latter, few people concerned mainly with teacher education contributed to courses beyond it, and only a tiny proportion of staff concerned mainly with BA and BSc degree work contributed to BEd or PGCE courses. This suggests that a potentially valuable contribution to initial training remains largely untapped. In the rare instances in which such staff were involved there was some useful work. In one polytechnic, for example, the quality of the humanities main subject component of the BEd degree course was significantly enriched by contributions of staff from other parts of the polytechnic, with particular areas of expertise in media studies and in anthropology.

In institutions offering diversified degree opportunities, it was often the case that staff were teaching BA, BSc and BEd students together, eg for education and some of the subject studies. Here, the fact that seminars served a dual purpose was sometimes an advantage as far as the BEd students were concerned; for example, when staff concerned with BA courses were able to contribute to discussions from a different standpoint. There was no doubt that the provision of diversified degrees made accessible to students in teacher training a wide range of staff well qualified in academic disciplines, and with scholarly interests which enhanced the undergraduate teaching for many BEd courses. However, difficulties of coordinating the work of larger numbers of staff, many of whom made only minor contributions to the course, had not always been successfully tackled.

This problem was well illustrated by one particular example in which no fewer than 120 members of staff contributed to the teaching of 390 BEd students and the course lacked proper progression and coherence.

The other main contribution of staff involved in initial training was to the in-service education of qualified teachers (INSET) and took the form either of short non-award-bearing courses or of more substantial courses leading to degree or diploma awards. The extent of participation in courses other than initial training courses, by staff primarily concerned with the latter, varied considerably. At the extremes, INSET accounted in one college of higher education for 44 per cent of the total of teacher education and in another for as little as 3 per cent. It was evident that contributions to INSET enriched initial training work, for example by helping tutors keep abreast of current developments, and by enabling their ideas to be tested against those of experienced teachers currently immersed in the day to day activities of schooling.

Quality in schools: the initial training of teachers

Although INSET was not a major focus of the survey, other ways in which it brought benefit to initial training students were often observed. There were, for instance, good examples of initial training students, serving teachers, and tutors working together in schools on a common project. Within the training institutions themselves there were often better facilities and displays where teaching rooms were used both for initial training and INSET courses than where these functions were separated. At one institution, work done by tutors and teachers on an INSET course on science was displayed in the college and later used in the PGCE course to enable students to appreciate how children in the primary school can be helped to develop an understanding of the concept of energy.

Academic qualifications

The great majority of the staff contributing to initial training were judged to be well qualified academically. Over two thirds possessed masters' degrees, either in education or in their own subject disciplines, and about 10 per cent were qualified at doctoral level. Almost all were qualified teachers. The 10 per cent or so who had never taught in schools included staff recruited specifically for diversified degree work who taught mainly on courses other than those in education. Such people were invariably highly qualified in their own subjects, and their contributions to initial training were almost exclusively in main subject studies, or occasionally in education studies, rather than in subject method or curriculum studies.

Most of the staff had been in post for a decade or longer, and the period following their appointments had seen a number of important changes in initial teacher training. In addition to the major changes referred to earlier, there has been increased emphasis on a number of key professional issues; for example, multi-ethnic education or special needs in the ordinary school. In particular, in several institutions there was a shortage of staff with expertise in the latter. There was, however, evidence of commendable attempts to help staff to make their qualifications more relevant to changing needs, and these are discussed later in the chapter. Some staff had, through their own personal initiatives, been able to develop new areas of knowledge and expertise, for example in the field of special educational needs or in aspects of primary school practice. In general, where qualifications were both of high academic standing and of relevance to current educational issues, there was evidence of stimulating and challenging work.

Teaching backgrounds

At the beginning of the survey approximately two thirds of the staff contributing to initial training courses had not held full-time teaching posts in schools during the previous ten years, and the great majority of their teaching experience had been in secondary schools. Because of the increasing emphasis on the training of teachers for junior and early years work, the school teaching experience of a large number of staff was therefore neither recent nor appropriate.

During the period of the survey most institutions were able to appoint a small number of tutors with recent and relevant experience of teaching in schools, and the voluntary colleges proved particularly successful in this. Nevertheless, by the time of the last of the visits, no more than 10 per cent of the staff throughout the sample had held a teaching post in a school during the previous three years.

There was some evidence that staff who had recently held posts in schools brought with them an enthusiasm and detailed knowledge of classroom practice and resources, and the contributions of these tutors were particularly valuable. There were some instances of such staff experiencing difficulties in making the transition from school teaching to teaching in higher education, and these may to some extent have reflected a lack of proper induction procedures in some institutions.

Several instances were noted where the lack of recent teaching experience, particularly in primary schools, appeared to put tutors at a disadvantage, for example in the selection of materials and teaching models, and there were cases where staff lacked the experience to provide effective advice to students on teaching practice. There were some good examples of tutors without primary school experience providing relevant and appropriate curriculum courses for the middle years group, but it was very unusual to find such examples for early years courses. Indeed, even where tutors had experience of teaching older junior children there were instances where the work provided for students training to teach very young children was not informed by an understanding of the best of current practice.

Staff deployment

The range of duties undertaken by individual tutors in all kinds of institutions was quite wide and included lectures, seminars, individual tutorial work, student counselling, supervision of teaching practice, and course development. The majority of lecturers were involved in most of these activities. More senior staff with major administrative responsibilities had a smaller involvement in some of these aspects, but often their work still reflected the full range.

In the majority of institutions the same tutorial team taught on the BEd and PGCE courses. Subject method and curriculum courses were usually taught separately to the different phase groups in both BEd and PGCE, and the same was true of professional studies where these were provided as a course in their own right. Education studies courses, including those which incorporated professional studies, were generally taught to combined groups of BEd students training for primary and secondary schools. Although combining the groups in this way made for some economies in the use of staff time, it was not always of educational advantage to the students, and some of the sessions seen lacked a clear focus.

Several institutions were able to deploy staff with primary expertise to teach the primary curriculum components, generally to good effect. A few cases were noted where staff with substantial or recent school experience were not as fully involved in curriculum and professional studies work as they might have been.

Staff were most effectively deployed when they worked cooperatively as a team with strong leadership and clearly defined responsibilities, making full use of their specific interests and expertise. There were numerous examples of such good practice at subject departmental level, but it was less usual to find it operating in a tutor team for the whole of a BEd or PGCE course. It is a task for management to consider ways in which closer cooperation can be achieved between staff teaching different components of the same course.

Involvement of visiting staff

All the survey institutions made some use of visiting staff in their initial training work, and about two thirds employed them extensively. Generally, the main purpose of such involvement was to supplement the range of expertise which could be offered by full-time staff, though it did on occasion serve other purposes too. Exchanges enabled staff members to extend or refresh their own experience (see also later Chapters), usually in local schools but occasionally in other institutions. In cases where the visiting teachers were from schools used for teaching practice, there were potential advantages for the supervision of students' work in schools. There were many examples of the value of this arrangement.

The employment of visiting staff took the following forms: joint appointment, temporary full-time appointment, temporary part-time appointment, and individual lecture or workshop session. By far the most ambitious and difficult mode of involving visiting staff was the joint appointment. The examples seen demonstrated the advantage of enabling the holder to maintain a concurrent grasp of two crucially related roles, notably those of college tutor and classroom teacher, but there were some instances of conflicting demands on time and personal commitment working to the disadvantage of one or both roles. Joint appointments did not appear as a feature in any of the polytechnics surveyed, and only five of the colleges had such arrangements. In one further case the administrative difficulties encountered at the planning stage had proved insuperable, and the appointment had not been made. In another instance there was a reasonably well established joint appointment where the role outside the college was not that of class teacher but of teachers' centre warden. Only one of the institutions, a voluntary college, enjoyed extensive and relatively long-term arrangements for joint appointments. Here, four specialists (one in mathematics, one in language development, one in modern languages and one in religious education) were based in the college's resource centres for just over half their time, contributing to course lecture and seminar work and spending just under half their time in an advisory capacity with local teachers. The response of the students indicated that these arrangements made a valuable contribution to work in the college.

Temporary secondment of serving teachers, often for a period of a year either on a full-time or part-time basis, was rather more common, perhaps because such arrangements are easier to achieve administratively than are joint appointments. Secondments were mainly for purposes other than involvement in initial training work; for example, for research projects or for advanced courses. Recently, the approval of arrangements for teacher fellowships has made it possible for teachers to be appointed to some of the institutions as teacher fellows. These temporary secondments served to bring recent or concurrent classroom experience into the college and as such were often valuable. In a few cases, a period of one academic year was insufficient for the teacher to adjust to teaching in a higher education context and for his/her experience of classroom work in school to be put to full use.

Eight of the institutions were making use of teachers seconded on a temporary basis from their posts in school. These teachers generally contributed to professional studies work with students preparing for primary school teaching, though three colleges used secondments to extend their special needs work. Four of the institutions, including two polytechnics, made use of both full-time and part-time secondments, the other four operating part-time secondments only. These arrangements were generally, though not invariably, successful. One of the more extensive and successful was that where the institution employed 12 carefully selected heads and teachers as teacher-tutors. All were well known to the institution's staff as all had previously attended substantial in-service courses there. They supervised students on teaching practice within their own schools, discussing progress with the students and with their tutors, who usually visited once or twice during each teaching practice.

By far the most common form of participation by visiting staff was the individual lecture or other one-off contributions. The examples encountered during the survey were judged on the whole to be quite useful, but their relevance to the needs of students varied rather more widely than that of the other uses of visiting staff. At its best the contribution of the visiting speaker served to inspire students and provided them with a fresh perspective on education. At its worst, it was a poor presentation either of ideas with which students were already familiar or of specialist material of little interest to the majority. Examples of the many useful sessions conducted by visiting speakers included one by a local teacher on uses of microcomputers in her school; one by a visiting head on values in children's literature; and one by a deputy county education officer on multi-ethnic education. Less successful were those by a teacher who spoke for an hour leaving little time for questions, by a head who did not organise the material effectively, and by a teachers' centre leader who went little beyond a surface description of matters not really relevant to the students' needs. The majority of single contributions by visiting staff were by people currently employed by local education authorities: teachers, heads, advisers, and educational psychologists. There were also a few contributions made by others concerned with education: members of health and social services professions, and representatives of parents' organisations. Some institutions could have done more to draw on the experience of a broader range of people who would bring different points of view: for example, school governors, members of voluntary agencies, parents, employers, businessmen, and politicians.

Some of the sessions conducted by visitors, while interesting in their own right and of general relevance to the training of teachers, were not effectively integrated into the particular programmes in which the students were engaged. This points to the need for careful planning to ensure that the speakers and the students are fully aware of the ways in which their topics fit within the course as a whole. In some of the work seen, it was apparent that preliminary discussions between organising tutors and visiting speakers would have resulted in more relevant material being more effectively presented.

Staff development policies

Those institutions which had clearly formulated staff development policies tended to focus upon only one or two of the many possible forms of staff development. Policy was broadly concerned with aspects of: induction of new staff; allowance of time for study and research; and arrangements for further experience in schools.

There was a variety of induction practices for new staff, the initiatives for these tending to be within particular subject or phase teams rather than the result of an institution-wide policy. One such programme, which appeared to work successfully, was arranged principally for teachers on temporary full-time secondment to the college but was extended to include newly appointed college tutors. In the same college, all new tutors were given induction in methods of supervising primary teaching practice. Another establishment involved newly-appointed early years tutors in regular team meetings with specialists in particular areas of the curriculum. In a few instances, induction policies focused on developing areas of the curriculum rather than on new staff. Among examples of staff seminars were some concerned with microelectronics, run by a lecturer who had recently completed a course in this field, some with language across the curriculum, and some with special needs.

All the institutions reported that their staff were encouraged to acquire further qualifications and to undertake research. The proportion of staff actually engaged in working towards advanced qualifications varied considerably, from 4 per cent in some institutions to over 30 per cent in others. Institutions generally supported staff attendance on full-time or part-time courses run elsewhere and leading to advanced qualifications, the initiatives for this appearing to stem from individuals rather than from staff development policies.

Over the period of the survey, there was a discernible change in the emphasis of staff development. The number of staff reported as being engaged in working towards advanced qualifications declined, as did the number reported as having full-time study leave. Generally, the decline in time spent on advanced study was balanced by an increase in time spent on work in schools. Here the evidence of an allocation of time governed by policy was much stronger. Over the period of the survey a number of institutions evolved arrangements designed to ensure that particular tutors, usually subject specialists, were each seconded for a substantial amount of time, generally a term, to gain or extend teaching experience in primary schools. Some institutions arranged for staff to teach regularly, eg on one day a week, in schools. By the end of the survey, the acquisition of such experience had clearly become a high priority for the majority of the institutions.

This changing emphasis in staff development emerged quite clearly during the period of the survey, though the indications are that the changes came more from responses to personal initiatives and to external pressures than from coordinated policies within the establishments themselves. There is clearly a need for such policies. The institutions should consider the whole range of staff development activities and ensure that the balance reflects the priority needs of the institution as well as those of individuals.

Research, writing and other professional activities

As has been indicated earlier, the majority of the academic staff in the survey institutions possessed higher degrees, mostly at master's level. Some had taken doctorates. Beyond higher degree work, the contribution to research and publication was not large and very few institutions carried externally funded research projects. There were, however, numerous instances of individuals with good records of research and publication in fields directly applicable to teacher education. These included reading behaviour, concept development in junior age children, microcomputers and mathematics in school, friendship groups and self-image, education in a multi-ethnic society, and oral and written activities for the primary classroom.

Examples of groups of people actively engaged in collaborative research, with some support through external funding, were confined largely to the polytechnics. Here there were indications of a positive association between active engagement in classroom-based research and high quality contributions to teacher training, since the research took the form of curriculum development projects within particular subject areas. In one establishment, a trio of drama tutors formed the core of a team involved in writing and editing school texts and contributing to international publications on drama and teacher education. In another, a group of social studies tutors was engaged in evaluating an LEA project on alternative curriculum strategies. In a third, members of the science team were involved in the institution's school science research project, which was gaining national recognition through its development work with microelectronics and science for disabled pupils.

Tutors were also involved in a variety of allied activities which drew on their educational expertise. Such activities included consultancy work in schools. In one institution, for example, more than two fifths of the staff were engaged in such work, including technology in schools, gymnastics in primary schools, poetry in primary schools, and the development of story-telling techniques. Some school-related activities had been initiated by tutors and included the development of teaching materials for use in special schools and computer-aided learning.

Publications produced by staff included books for children, textbooks for school pupils and students, journal articles, and book reviews, and some had produced music recordings and video tapes. Among the art and music tutors were practitioners who had exhibited their work or published compositions.

In addition to study for further qualifications, research and consultancy, there was a wide range of activities which institutions recognised as staff development. These included work with the Health Education Council, project evaluation, external examining, directing courses, membership of professional associations, course validation, exchanges with overseas institutions, and preparation of computer software. Some staff were able to give their students a national or international perspective through their own professional involvement and contacts outside the institution and the locality.

Refreshment and extension of teaching experience

Supervision of students' teaching practice and other forms of school experience made it possible for tutors to sustain an interchange of ideas with practising teachers. Consultancy work in schools was fairly common, and this too was proving a useful means of keeping in touch as was the extensive commitment to INSET, discussed earlier. There were other forms of contact with schools. For example, tutors in two colleges worked on a part-time basis for their LEAs as religious education advisers; elsewhere a tutor acted as leader of the LEA curriculum development centre for physical education; in yet another college four staff were seconded to outside agencies. In some instances, children came into the training institution to be taught by members of staff.

The most powerful means of refreshment and extension of teaching skills for tutors was through regular periods of direct classroom teaching experience. By the end of the survey there was clear evidence that in almost all the institutions at least some members of staff were making use of this kind of experience as a means of refreshing their classroom teaching skills. Though this development had begun prior to the survey, it had undoubtedly been stimulated considerably by the publication of the Government's criteria for initial training.

Most of the institutions reported that a proportion of staff, up to a fifth, were regularly teaching for half a day to a day a week in school. A number seconded tutors to schools on a one-term basis. Some institutions were not able to sustain what were initially high levels of involvement; in one, for example, two fifths of the staff were reported as being engaged at the beginning of the survey, but by the end of the survey pressure on staffing had, in their view, made it necessary to reduce this to a quarter. In other instances, however, despite staffing difficulties, the level of staff involvement had increased. It was not possible to ascertain the extent to which direct experience of classroom teaching was a voluntary 'extra' or was recognised as part of the staff's workloads. Almost invariably their work took place in primary schools, understandably in view of many tutors' relative lack of experience in the primary phase, and it tended to be in the tutors' own specialist subject areas. It was said to be occurring in most areas of the curriculum, though mathematics and science seemed to be the most common.

Observation of tutors teaching in schools was not a feature of the survey. Many of those engaged in regular experience in schools appear to have worked as supernumeraries, and this may have placed limitations on the responsibilities they were likely to undertake, though there were instances of other arrangements. One tutor, for example, undertook an exchange with the deputy head of a junior school. In another college, religious education and science tutors exchanged classes with teachers for half a day weekly. Some of the classroom experience was hastily and perhaps haphazardly arranged, and institutions had not yet developed a means of assessing the most useful ways of giving it effect. It was clear that there was considerable room for expansion in the involvement of tutors in classroom teaching, and for contact which was more sustained, structured, and accountable than was evident from the survey. Development policies produced by the institutions will in future ensure that staff are able to gain such experience more extensively and in a wider variety of forms.

Counselling and guidance of students

At all the institutions each student was assigned a personal tutor, who was usually responsible both for professional and academic guidance and for personal welfare. In some instances separate tutors took responsibility for each role. The amount of time allocated to tutorial provision varied from one institution to another. At some there were regular timetabled sessions; at others, students saw their tutors only for a formal review each term or year, unless they had a personal need. At most polytechnics there were also professional counsellors whose services were available to the whole student population, and some colleges had also made such appointments.

In the majority of institutions, students stayed with the same tutor throughout the course, unless they requested otherwise, but in some there was a change at the end of the first year of the BEd course. There were a few instances where students had experienced many changes of tutor because of staff reductions, and some were unclear who their tutor was. Others felt that the tutor's workload, and responsibility for a growing number of students (sometimes 25-30), reduced the effectiveness of the system. Where counselling was not a timetabled activity, its frequency and the time spent upon it depended on the commitment of the individual tutor. Institutions were beginning to take account of this and were seeking to move towards a more formal recognition of counselling duties.

Within the constraints described, the counselling and pastoral care provided by those staff concerned with it in the institutions were generally good. It was particularly supportive in respect of the students' work in schools. Where students had spent a period in school during the first year of a BEd course they were usually given an assessment of their progress. One institution set aside a week at the end of the first year when all the students received detailed guidance and counselling from all relevant tutors, and two days at the end of the second year for a similar exercise. Some institutions had review boards, before which students had to appear if they had failed courses or performed unsatisfactorily on teaching practice.

Validation

Validation, which is conducted by the Council for National Academic Awards (CNAA) and by a number of universities, is concerned with establishing the academic standards of a proposed course and ensuring that the institution is competent to offer and to teach it. It is not in itself a guarantee of standards.

The CNAA is responsible for validating courses in 13 of the survey institutions, and it shares validation with universities in the case of 5 more. As part of the validation process the CNAA expects institutions to prepare a detailed statement of aims and objectives for the course, its structure, syllabuses, procedures for examination and assessment, details of the qualifications and experience of staff, systems of course control and management, and the methods by which the course will be evaluated as it proceeds. Almost without exception, the survey institutions associated with CNAA found preparations for validation a highly time-consuming process, placing a heavy burden on top of existing teaching duties. Some of the best courses seen, however, had emerged from thorough and systematic course development.

In many cases, the documentation produced by the colleges for university validation was similar to that prepared for CNAA submissions. A consistent difference between the expectations of the CNAA and the universities lay in the emphasis placed by the latter upon subject studies and education studies rather than upon the professional and curriculum work or the overall coherence of the course. A small number of universities laid down a common course structure, or specified the nature of assessment and the timing of examinations for all their colleges. Sometimes colleges found this to be a serious constraint on course design.

Many lecturers valued the ease of opportunity to contact their opposite numbers in the universities to discuss modifications to approved courses, or approaches which might be adopted in proposed new courses. Such informal contacts enabled a professional dialogue to be established which usually continued after validation, but these separate discussions invariably took place with little reference to the degree course as a whole. There were a few examples of piecemeal validation where the process of considering components separately had repercussions upon the coherence of the course as a whole. For example, in one institution the different requirements set for individual subjects led to major inconsistencies between parallel components of the same course, and in another instance a college was allowed to recruit students to follow a course, parts of which had not been approved by the validating body.

Although careful documentation was not in itself a guarantee of an effective course the following were features which were common to all courses that were proving effective: the documentation was derived from consultation between all the staff responsible for coordinating the various components of the course; all the staff were committed to what it contained; and in spirit and substance it influenced the teaching of the course. Such features were the result of good leadership by those responsible for the course within the institution.

Resources

In almost all the institutions, teacher training took place in purpose-built or specifically adapted accommodation. Where there had been amalgamations this was usually in the premises of the former college of education. Rationalising the use of accommodation sometimes proved difficult, and in half the survey institutions the teacher training work was on two or more sites. Few of the colleges which had been amalgamated were close together and thus in many institutions staff or students had to travel between sites for different parts of their work, or, conversely, there was uneconomical duplication of teaching. Split-site working was recognised as far from ideal but was sometimes unavoidable when it was found impossible to centralise expensive specialist facilities for particular subjects, such as home economics, physical education or science. Furthermore, the number of students was sometimes too large to be accommodated on a single site. At the extreme, in one institution a third of the students were on a campus 25 miles from its main site.

Much of the teaching accommodation was situated on attractive well-tended campuses with residential and leisure facilities to hand. Some of the buildings were very modern: one college opened in 1972 and another had benefited from a major building programme in 1978. On the other hand some premises were over 100 years old, but where they had been carefully modernised and adapted they offered an excellent environment for teacher education.

A good deal of the accommodation used for the initial training of teachers was designed for secondary work and many of the specialist subject facilities were good. At their best they included suites of rooms which provided a natural meeting and working place for staff and students and a focal point for the subject, complete with resources and attractive displays of work. Colleges with a long tradition of primary work had, in general, developed their facilities and resources to reflect the best practice in schools and to give students experiences which provided good models for their own teaching. Two of these colleges had adapted some of their older accommodation to replicate the facilities and atmosphere of a lively primary school. These provided not only a stimulating environment for professional training but also an ideal place to which young children could be brought to work in small groups with the students. In contrast, some colleges which had moved from a strong secondary tradition into primary training had not succeeded in modifying their accommodation to meet the new demands. The survey showed clearly that the quality of the working environment was important in the training of teachers, and that suitably furnished rooms with good display and ready access to resources contributed significantly to the quality of the students' learning.

In a quarter of the institutions serious deficiencies were noted in the accommodation, and the fabric of a number of buildings was deteriorating through lack of maintenance. The situation was noticeably bad where teacher training classes took place in general rooms which were not the responsibility of any particular department or member of staff. Some of these rooms were so poorly decorated and maintained, so bleak and lacking in facilities and display, that it was difficult for even the most imaginative tutor to provide a good model for students in these conditions.

Most of the institutions were judged to have adequate libraries, some of them outstanding. One polytechnic library mainly devoted to teacher education possessed a carefully maintained and balanced collection of 150,000 volumes, subscribed to 800 journals, and held about 30,000 books and other materials for use in school. Even in small colleges, 90,000 volumes in the main collection and subscription to 400 periodicals were not uncommon. Where institutions had been amalgamated it was not unusual to find several libraries. In one polytechnic, students had access to six, each with a different specialist emphasis. Computerised links between the libraries for cataloguing and issue added to their effective use and enabled books to be transferred to where they were needed by readers. By and large, collections were up to date and relevant, but some libraries were strongly biased towards the former secondary courses, and primary materials were inadequate to support the current work. There was a need for selective pruning of some of the collections.

Most libraries were open into the evening on weekdays, but most were closed at weekends. Only one college had a full service on Saturdays and reading facilities on Sundays. For the most part, librarians seemed conscious of the need for library hours to reflect rather than determine the pattern of the students' work. Although libraries generally had adequate working space for students, expanding collections of both books and non-book materials were beginning to put a strain on the accommodation in several institutions. Students' work did not always reveal as much reference to books and periodicals as might have been expected from the generous provision of many of the libraries. In contrast, teaching practice libraries were normally well used by students to support their work in schools.

In addition to their library facilities, over a quarter of the survey institutions had developed specialist resource centres, for example in microelectronics, religious education, reading, music and mathematics. One college had nine such centres and two others housed the more general local teachers' centres. Often the centres had been established as places to which serving teachers could come to examine books, materials and apparatus, in addition to serving the needs of initial training students.

The structure of courses

BEd courses in the institutions generally consisted of five elements which throughout this report are termed subject studies, curriculum studies, education studies, professional studies, and school experience. PGCE courses contained all these components except subject studies, which the students were deemed to have completed in their undergraduate courses.

Subject studies in BEd in most institutions had two major purposes: they provided students with higher education at a personal level and they contributed to their professional repertoire. To students training for secondary schools they gave a specialist teaching subject, and to intending primary teachers an additional strength in a particular area of the curriculum. The curriculum studies components both of BEd and PGCE courses were designed to have different functions according to phase. In secondary courses this component focused on the methodology of the students' specialist subject(s); in primary courses it attempted to span the whole curriculum, or a substantial part of it, providing the student with some knowledge of each of the areas as well as the methods of teaching them. Education studies and professional studies, often linked in a single strand (for example, with the title Teaching Studies), aimed to provide a theoretical background to teaching and learning, to give students a better understanding of the context in which pupils' learning takes place, and to help them draw on this knowledge in developing their teaching skills. School experience included all types of student involvement with children in schools. In addition to substantial periods of block practice most courses also provided serial experience comprising a half day or day per week over several weeks. In many cases children were brought into the institution to provide students with opportunities for work with individuals or groups of various sizes.

Most of the institutions had adopted a concurrent approach to training in which, broadly speaking, the students encountered all these components side by side. In some instances the elements were spread evenly across the whole course; in others the emphasis on particular elements varied at different stages. In one case the third year was entirely devoted to professional work and school experience, even though both featured at other periods in the course.

By the end of the survey, two-thirds of the BEd courses comprised only the four-year honours route, while the remainder had been planned to enable students to complete the unclassified degree before proceeding to honours or, at least, to delay a decision until later in the third year. Not infrequently, this formula resulted in a final year of academic work, usually in subject studies and education studies, and in some cases school experience either played a minor part or was absent altogether. In a few BEd courses students were required to qualify for honours at the end of the first or second year, after which the unclassified and honours programmes divided.

At the start of the survey the institutions offering both primary and secondary training through the BEd degree taught the students jointly for part of their course. Frequently, work in the specialist subject and in education studies was common to both primary and secondary students while curriculum courses were generally separate. By the end of the survey several institutions no longer provided secondary training in the BEd, and most of the others had approval to offer only a few secondary subjects. Consequently, in only about a quarter of the BEd subject studies courses were primary and secondary students taught together, though this practice continued widely in education studies.

Amalgamations which brought former colleges of education into polytechnics offered opportunities for joint teaching between initial training and other undergraduate courses. These were exemplified in the survey institutions, a number of which specifically designed their programmes so that students could delay their decision to train as teachers. The operation of the Diploma of Higher Education (Dip HE) to this end is described in Chapter 5. In some institutions one or more years of joint teaching of an academic subject for students on the BEd and other degree courses were used as a means of making it possible to transfer between courses at the end of that time. Throughout the survey period about half the BEd specialist subject studies courses offered to secondary students and a third of those offered to primary students were taught jointly with other degrees. Even where delayed choice of degree was not a major objective, the larger teaching groups created by joint teaching had enabled some institutions to offer a more extensive range of subjects in the BEd course than might otherwise have been possible with a limited number of students. In many such courses BEd students were in a small minority. This rarely presented a problem for secondary students, but the selection of content, often limited by other elements of the BEd timetable, rarely provided intending primary teachers with an adequate background of knowledge which could inform and support their teaching in school. Lecturing, usually undertaken by well qualified staff, was often of a high calibre, but there were instances of an expository style of teaching being used intensively, sometimes unremittingly, and this did not offer intending teachers a good model for their own teaching. During periods of teaching practice, BEd students sometimes missed part of the course, and special arrangments, often *ad hoc,* had to be made to fill in the gaps.

A small number of BEd courses were organised on a modular basis. Although this arrangement allowed students a wider choice it was more difficult to achieve coherence and establish links between the parts of the course. This problem was particularly acute in one BEd (based on a Dip HE) with 123 modules in the first two years, varying in length from 7 to 68 hours. Planning was a complex task, demands on students were excessive, and too much was expected of some very short modules. Conversely, courses with fewer modules, comprising the equivalent of half a term's work or more, tended to be more coherent.

Whatever the overall structure, most BEd courses were planned with about 30 teaching weeks in each year. The final year was often somewhat shorter, to allow for examinations and assessment. A major element of all courses was the time given to school experience, which was normally 15 to 16 weeks in a three-year unclassified degree and about 20 weeks in a four-year honours degree (see Chapter 8 for more details). Class contact hours varied a great deal, from 12 to 20 hours per week; in the fourth year some courses had less class contact time and placed more emphasis on independent study. In addition to attending classes and visiting schools, students were expected to spend considerable time in private study. Most of the institutions claimed this to be at least equal to the time spent in class, and sometimes double or more.

The PGCE course provides an intensive period of training which comprises curriculum studies, education and professional studies, and school experience, all completed in one year. By the end of the survey, most institutions had moved towards the expected length of 36 weeks. The time devoted to block school experience varied between 11 and 16 weeks, but almost all the courses included other opportunities for students to work in schools. The number of hours of class contact during the college based part of the course was generally between 300 and 350 overall. This barely provided sufficient time to cover all that was required in professional training, particularly for the primary phase. However, for many students the number of class hours per week was substantially more than in their undergraduate courses.

Subject studies

All BEd secondary courses devoted a significant proportion of time to specialist subject studies, which commonly took up half or more of the total time for the degree: between 600 and 700 hours for the first subject and 300 hours or more for the second subject. Practical subjects often had rather more contact time: home economics and physical education, for example, sometimes exceeded 1000 hours in a four-year course. In a few institutions insufficient time was devoted to a second subject to provide a satisfactory foundation for teaching in the secondary school. In primary courses the study of the specialist subject(s) was allocated on average 350 hours in three-year courses and 420 hours in honours courses, but the extremes ranged from 135 hours to almost 600 hours. The Northern Ireland institutions were at the upper extreme of this range. For the most part, the allocation of time to specialist subject study for those intending to be primary teachers was inadequate to meet their needs.

Most institutions allowed primary students to choose from at least six subjects, and some offered 12 or more. Where there was joint teaching with other degree courses a larger number of subjects was often available. At the beginning of the survey not all these were directly related to the primary curriculum, eg business studies, but by the end of the survey over 85 per cent of students were studying subjects related to those which are universally found in the primary school curriculum. Thus, nearly half were taking humanities courses (including English, geography, history and religious education) 17 per cent expressive arts (art, drama, music), 10 per cent science (mainly biology), 7 per cent mathematics and 4 per cent physical education. Of the remaining 15 per cent, almost 6 per cent were studying social sciences and 3 per cent were taking French.

In those institutions offering secondary BEd courses, over 40 per cent of the students were taking physical education (or a related subject) and 22 per cent home economics as a first subject. By contrast only 8 per cent of students were studying craft, design and technology, 7 per cent mathematics, 6 per cent religious education and science, and fewer than 2 per cent music. Recruitment to the secondary BEd had become more difficult by the end of the survey. 95 per cent of the available places had been filled for the 1984 intake, but there was a shortfall in mathematics, science, religious education and music, and institutions had over-recruited to physical education by 19 per cent. Figure 3 overleaf shows the distribution of primary and secondary BEd students, and Figure 4 on page 51 the relationship between target numbers and enrolments for the secondary BEd in 1984.

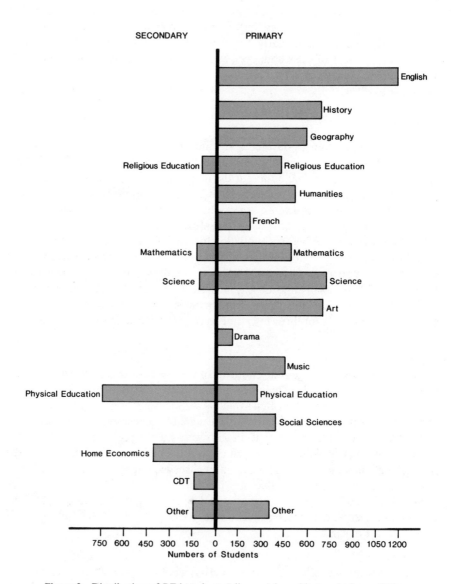

Figure 3 Distribution of BEd students (all years) by subject and phase, 1984.

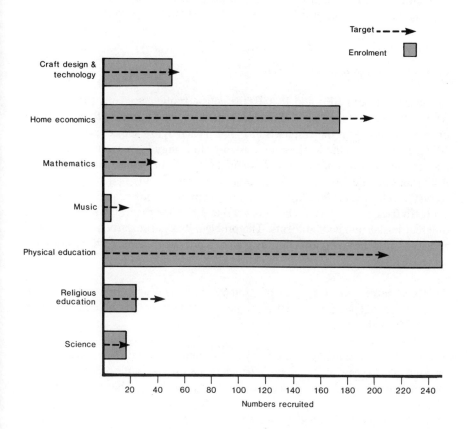

Figure 4   Secondary BEd – target numbers and enrolments, 1984.

Frequently, the demands of the work in specialist subject studies for secondary students were intellectually challenging and comparable with those of the second year of conventional subject degrees. As outlined above, all secondary students additionally took a methodology course on the teaching of the subject, and most of these were substantial. In contrast, it was unusual to find in primary BEd degrees specific courses which considered the application of the student's special subject(s) to the learning needs of primary school children and such courses were almost totally absent from the PGCE. This was a serious shortcoming, and a lost opportunity to help students develop a curricular strength based on their particular subject study. In the best examples, classroom applications of academic material were taught through organised links between a particular subject and an associated primary method course, or included as a component in the specialist subject part of the course.

Curriculum studies and subject method

In the case of both BEd and PGCE, the course training students for secondary schools emphasised the role of the subject specialism and normally focused on one or two subjects, with the emphasis in PGCE generally on subject pedagogy. For BEd students the methodology course usually ran alongside the main subject work, and the extent to which the two were integrated or related varied between institutions. Difficulties sometimes occurred when students had to choose their second or subsidiary subject from a list which contained none related to their recent study. In these circumstances the tutors had to adjust their teaching to cater for the different backgrounds of students. The problem was particularly acute in PGCE courses, where there was little time available to provide students with the necessary subject background which they might lack.

As noted earlier, most courses of primary training sought to respond to the expectation that the primary teacher should be able to cover the whole curriculum in relation to both content and teaching method.

Mathematics and language were invariably compulsory, but there were no such guarantees in the case of the others. When the survey began, some other subjects, for example science, were offered as options in many institutions, but by the end such options had largely been replaced by compulsory courses. It was rare for primary students with greater knowledge of a subject, and particularly those taking it as an academic study to be taught separately. Indeed, students entering most of the curriculum courses had a wide variety of backgrounds; some had achieved A-level or higher while others had only a minimal knowledge, having given up formal study of certain subjects before the end of their secondary education.

Education studies and professional studies

Education studies took up a significant proportion of the students' time in all BEd and PGCE courses, and while the average in BEd was about 100 hours per year, the range was from 60 hours per year to over 150 hours. The mean for one year PGCE courses was 86 hours (about a quarter of the course), but there was considerable variation, from 24 hours to 130 hours. Only a little over a quarter of the institutions provided separate education courses for primary and secondary students. In others, much of the content was common to both groups, especially at postgraduate level, but the students were often divided according to phase for seminars.

In approximately one third of BEd courses, education studies was taught quite separately from other parts of the course. In the remaining two-thirds it was most common to find education studies linked in some way with professional studies, though examples of complete integration were rare. It was also unusual to find education studies linked with main subject or curriculum study. There were, however, a number of instances of tutors establishing their own informal links between various parts of the course. In PGCE courses education studies was more often taught separately; where links existed they were usually with the main subject for secondary students.

It was rare to find any undergraduate courses described overtly as teaching the contributory disciplines of psychology, sociology, philosophy, history and curriculum studies throughout all the years of the course. A common pattern was for the course to be described as 'thematic' in years one and two, with an inter-disciplinary core, leading to options between discrete disciplines in the third year. These led to further discipline-based options in the fourth year. In the event, a large number of the inter-disciplinary or thematic courses proved to be either totally discipline-based in both content and staffing, or consisted of discrete topics each of which ran as a separate component for a few weeks. The emphasis placed upon the disciplines seemed most commonly to result from the specialist interests of those teaching the course. Thus the same topic taught by different people might take on a psychological or philosophical slant according to the perspective adopted by the tutor. Fourth year honours courses most commonly consisted of either the study of a single option or a core course plus an option. Very few continued with inter-disciplinary approaches, and it was rare to find project work in schools as an integral component. Postgraduate courses commonly comprised a series of topics each of which occupied the education studies sessions for one week. Some institutions successfully combined these topics into themes and a number taught a core course to which options could be added.

In varying degrees, all the institutions devoted attention to such professional issues as class organisation and control, setting and mixed ability teaching, assessment, record keeping, and other skills and knowledge essential to a teacher. While some institutions offered a separate strand of the course concerned with such matters, others incorporated them in education studies. In a few, attention to these issues was the responsibility of all tutors. This arrangement was successful only where there was an overall plan and adequate monitoring of what had been covered. Most training courses included substantial options in the education of children with special needs and in ethnic diversity. By the end of the survey period the majority of courses had also incorporated both these areas within either education studies or professional studies as a compulsory element for all students, though coverage was sometimes limited.

School experience

All courses provided block placements in schools of several weeks each, and most also offered some form of serial experience, a half day or whole day per week for a period of time. By the end of the survey, in most BEd courses there were between 80 and 100 days of school experience, while in PGCE courses there were usually between 70 and 90 days. The range was wide: for example, one three-year BEd included 50 days in school, a quite inadequate allocation, while one four year BEd allocated 127 days. The proportion of all school experience in BEd courses devoted to serial attachment varied from over 40 per cent to as little as 5 per cent; the average was approximately 20 per cent (16-20 days) and this seemed a reasonable figure. Most PGCE courses allocated about 25 per cent of the school-based time to this form of experience.

Serial experience usually aimed to give students the opportunity to focus on a specific topic, or some aspect of teaching closely related to the course, and to plan and discuss the experience with their peers as well as their tutors. This was at its most successful when students were given specific tasks to carry out on regular visits to school, which were then discussed in a follow-up seminar. Good links with education and professional studies were sometimes achieved in this way, particularly in PGCE courses.

There was considerable variation in the duration and timing of blocks of teaching practice in both BEd and PGCE courses, although the pattern of the practices was usually related to the structure of the course. It could also be affected by the number of students; the geographical distribution of placements; the number of schools used by the college; the proximity of other training establishments; and the staff available for supervision. In some institutions externally determined dates for BEd examinations, or joint teaching of BEd with BA/BSc students, also constrained the timing of school experience.

Within BEd courses, institutions generally offered students three main teaching practice blocks, together with interspersed periods of serial experience. Most courses were designed to give students substantial experience in schools at an early point in their training. This served the dual function of giving them a secure introduction to the classroom and helping to identify those who had made an inappropriate choice of career. Students were frequently critical of courses which did not provide this opportunity. It was rare to find block teaching practices in all four years of an honours course. The majority of those BEd courses which offered honours to students who successfully completed a fourth year after a three-year ordinary degree did not include substantial school experience in the final year. This arrangement has the serious disadvantage, among others, of creating a long period between the final school practice and the first appointment as a probationary teacher.

Where BEd students were taught alongside those on other degree courses, block teaching practices needed to be carefully timed if the students were not to miss lectures and tutorials. This presented few problems in those institutions which arranged suitable work placements for all students, whatever their degree course. But others had to take such steps as scheduling the block teaching practices for the beginning or end of a term, thereby restricting the time available and affecting the nature of the school experience.

Most institutions expected PGCE students to spend a brief period in a school before the course started. Within the course itself one short and one long practice were common, the main variation being one short and two medium length practices.

Some institutions were more successful than others in designing courses in which the timing of serial and block school experiences related well to the content of courses. These arrangements took account of the students' growing expertise and included a variety of schools and catchment areas. They also made the best use of the school year and the college year and more evenly distributed the supervision duties of tutors. The diagrams in Figure 5 between pages 56-60 illustrate some of the different BEd and PGCE course structures found among the institutions at the start of the survey.

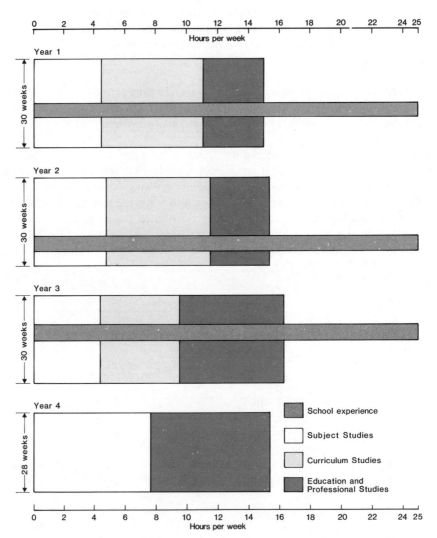

Figure 5a Primary BEd course
A concurrent pattern of training with parallel courses in subject studies, curriculum studies and education and professional studies throughout the first three years interspersed with periods of block practice in schools. There is no block experience in the final year.

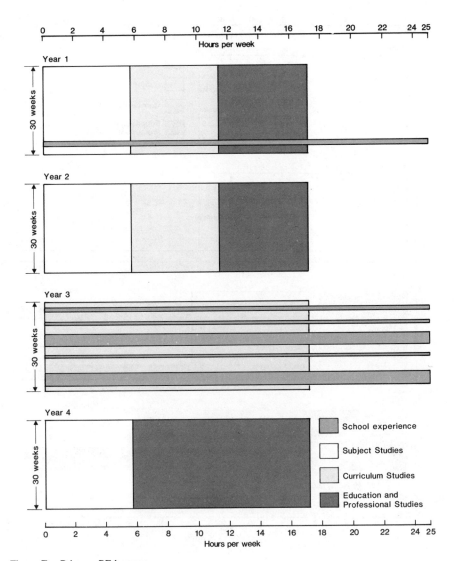

Figure 5b Primary BEd course
In this model the third year is devoted almost entirely to the professional elements although they do appear elsewhere in the course. In some cases the subject studies courses are common to BA/BSc programmes.

57

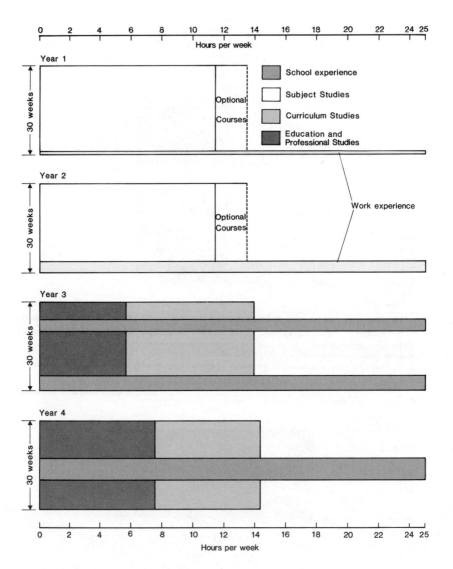

Figure 5c Post DipHE primary BEd course
This is a 2+2 structure with the professional elements of education and professional studies, curriculum studies and school experience confined to years 3 and 4. Other work experience is included at the DipHE stage. Students can delay their choice of career until at least the second year.

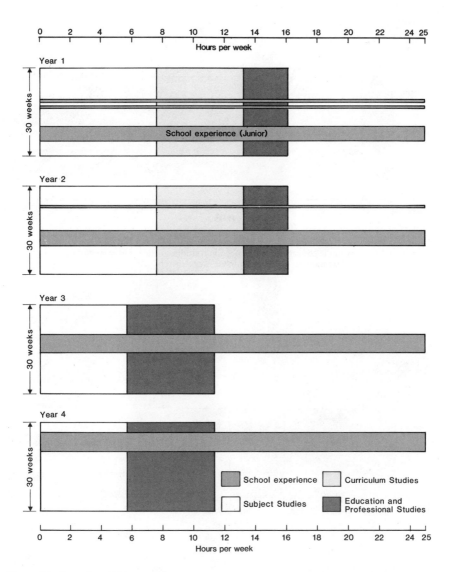

Figure 5d Secondary BEd course
In this model there is a strong emphasis on subject studies. There is a period of block school experience in each year and no possibility of leaving at the end of the third year with an unclassified BEd degree award. Curriculum studies cover a second teaching subject and issues such as special needs and multi-ethnic education.

59

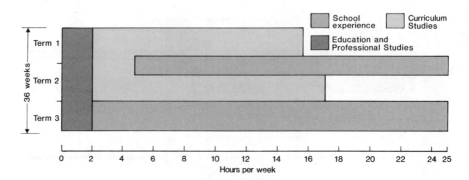

Figure 5e Primary PGCE course
In this example education and professional studies form a minor part of the course. At no time do the students spend a complete week in school.

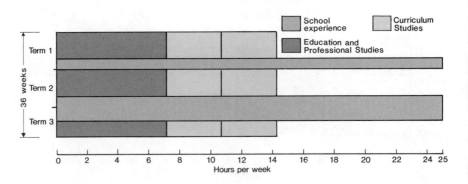

Figure 5f Secondary PGCE course
In this example curriculum studies covers two teaching subjects with equal allocations of time.

5 The training of primary teachers: the primary school curriculum

Context

Initial training for intending primary teachers was provided in all the 30 institutions included in the survey. The courses covered both the primary and the middle years and generally allowed students to focus on specific bands within this age range, such as 3 to 7, 4 to 9, 5 to 11 or 8 to 13 years. In structure and in content they represented the variety of courses available to students who choose to prepare for teaching in primary schools. The findings reported in this chapter draw on visits to 30 BEd courses and to 23 PGCE courses.

The training institutions generally sought to prepare students as general class teachers able to cover a broad curriculum. Many also believed that intending primary teachers need the knowledge and confidence which will give them a strength in one subject or area of the curriculum and which can also provide a foundation for the development of consultancy skills in the future, but this was addressed in only a minority of courses. This chapter examines the ways in which training institutions set about these tasks and also the extent to which the students were acquiring an understanding of the essential knowledge, concepts, skills and attitudes associated with the various areas of the curriculum which they will teach, and an appreciation of methods of teaching them.

Selection of students

BEd courses

The majority of candidates seeking a place on a BEd primary course had done so while completing their studies at school or at a college of further education (FE). Some had decided to delay their entry for a year or two and deferred an application until they were 19 or 20 years of age. For others, particularly women, the decision to become a teacher had been left until much later, and they entered courses as mature students. More than four-fifths of the BEd students were under 21 years of age when they began their training, and a similar proportion were female. In seven of the institutions in England and Wales students wishing to take a BEd course first pursued a diploma of higher education course (DipHE). In five cases the DipHE was a 'free-standing' qualification which enabled students to transfer to any degree course offered by the institution on successful completion of the two-year course. In the other two, the DipHE was awarded to appropriately competent students who, having embarked on a BEd, decided to discontinue their studies after the two-year stage. Enrolment on a free-standing DipHE permitted the student to delay a firm decision about teaching as a career and also, for some, gave a further two years to meet the mathematics and/or English language requirement for entry to initial training. In one institution as many as a quarter of the students who entered the DipHE phase, and who were firmly committed to becoming teachers, began without an acceptable O-level grade in mathematics. In order to qualify for the BEd phase they acquired the qualification by attending a course outside the institution or by taking a DipHE unit recognised as an equivalent qualification.

Where candidates do not meet the normal entry requirements, the regulations of the validating bodies make provision for their admission if they are mature (generally over the age of 21 or, in some cases, 23) and if they are able to offer experience or other qualifications which make them suitable for the course. This may be through a mature matriculation examination, the possession of qualifications such as those for nursing, or success in a specially designed 'access' course. There was clear evidence that some institutions, notably those with CNAA validation, had taken considerable advantage of such arrangements. Six of the survey institutions had linked access courses. Access courses are designed to enable a wider range of students to enter higher education, and may be linked to more than one institution or devised in relation to one particular outlet. Those encountered in the survey were usually offered by a college of further education, with the course content agreed with the associated teacher training institution. Some had been designed with the ethnic minority communities particularly in mind. Tutors from the training institutions helped in the selection of students from the access course and, although there was no automatic right of entry to the BEd, successful candidates from an access course usually did gain a BEd place.

Students had been alerted to the range of BEd courses available in a number of ways: by national and local advertising, by the staff of the institutions responding to requests to give talks in schools, and by the institutions' own prospectuses. Generally, the descriptions of the courses were clear, and candidates were given a good indication of their special features and the facilities and opportunities available, though it was rare for there to be an indication of what qualities might be looked for at interview. Few institutions required passes in specific A-level subjects, though there was evidence that most students with standard qualifications did have an A-level pass appropriate to their subject study. A few institutions set considerable store by the reports from the referees, whose judgements were used to eliminate some candidates without an interview taking place. In one college, reports were sought from the heads of the schools where candidates had had experience of working with children, a practice which deserves to be adopted more widely.

The academic qualifications of applicants accepted for BEd primary courses in relation to the total undergraduate population were not high. Of those admitted on the basis of GCE, about a third had three passes at A-level, and a half had two; a typical profile was two passes at grade C and one at D, which represents an A-level points score of five. Of the remainder, two-thirds had qualifications deemed equivalent to A-level, and one-third were 'special entry' students, ie older candidates, not possessing A-level or its equivalent. In Northern Ireland, where there is keener competition to gain a BEd place, the average A-level points score was just over six.

In the survey institutions, no candidate was admitted to a BEd course without an interview and this was seen by candidates and institutions alike as the most important aspect of the selection process. Typically, before candidates were invited for interview, their application forms and references were scrutinised by senior staff. They looked for evidence of experience with children or young people, predictions about academic potential, and the match between the applicant's academic record to date and the chosen course of study. The institutions recognised that candidates attending for interview had to decide whether they in turn liked the institution and what it had to offer. All of them took considerable care to ensure that candidates were shown round by students and given every opportunity, in as relaxed an atmosphere as was possible, to make personal judgements about the social environment as well as the nature of the course.

Selection interviews usually lasted about 30 minutes and were normally conducted by at least two tutors. In those interviews attended, the occasion was generally used to explore the candidate's personal and academic qualities and to assess motivation. It was usually felt to be impossible during a short interview to make formal assessments, and any grading was confined to general suitability, intellectual potential, and written and spoken expression. In judging personal qualities, those conducting the interview looked for attributes such as enthusiasm, perceptiveness, common sense, firmness, sensitivity, and friendliness. Many institutions invited serving teachers to take part in at least some of the interviews, and a few had long-standing arrangements to involve them in the process of selection. Apart from some practical tests in music and physical education, candidates for primary courses in the survey institutions appeared to have no opportunities to demonstrate their capabilities beyond the confines of the interview.

PGCE courses

Competition for places on PGCE primary courses has been strong for several years, with at least three applicants for every primary place. Throughout the period of the survey, the institutions offering PGCE were able to reach their target numbers with ease, though only a few men were recruited. The majority of students had degrees which related closely to aspects of the primary school curriculum, but there were instances of degrees which could not be considered appropriate. The candidates themselves did not always realise the importance of having a teaching subject to offer. There was some evidence of institutions selecting students in such a way as to ensure a wide ranging mix of curricular specialisms, and they accepted that, in a few instances, this might lead to the rejection of a candidate who in other respects would have been considered suitable for training.

The institutions sought to recruit students with a high degree of commitment to working with children or young people, and they generally looked for the same personal qualities as those they required for entry to undergraduate courses. Evidence of hobbies, interests and skills, such as swimming, sports and games, was considered an advantage. For early years work, creative or musical ability and a flair for working imaginatively were particularly valued. One institution required evidence of an interest in multi-ethnic issues and favoured candidates who had worked with ethnic minority groups or who could speak a community language. Every candidate for admission to this institution, irrespective of previous qualifications, had to demonstrate proficiency in written English by writing an essay on the day of the interview.

Applications were usually assessed by a primary phase tutor, and normally candidates were not invited for interview until references had been received, generally from the candidate's personal tutor during his or her period as an undergraduate. Candidates selected to attend were generally expected to show a degree of confidence, maturity and a professional attitude at the interview, which was particularly concerned with probing commitment, motivation, and experience. The interviews sometimes involved practising teachers, and in one institution the participation of teachers had been extended by requiring candidates to carry out a series of teaching tasks organised by the teachers in their own schools. The activities included reading stories, coaching games, or organising and supervising art activities with a group of children. Tutors and school staff were able to observe the candidates at work and this evidence contributed to the decision about whether a place should be offered. Effective initiatives of this kind deserve to be more widely used in the system.

The primary school curriculum

Curriculum studies

Equipping teachers with the full range of desirable capabilities constitutes a formidable challenge for those tutors who are responsible for course design. Not least among the problems is the need to provide a reasonable allocation of time for each of the competing priorities, a matter which has been discussed in Chapter 3. The institutions offered a variety of routes to professional competence, though the range was so wide as to be a cause for concern. The students' capacity to cope with most aspects of the primary curriculum was largely developed through a number of curriculum courses of relatively short duration. Typically, most of these were within a compulsory core, though in a number of cases some important elements were optional.

Institutions which sought to give students a teaching strength in a subject or in an area of the curriculum usually built this around the students' specialist subject studies in the BEd course. Broadly speaking, specialist subject studies with associated pedagogical studies were provided in two ways. The first was in the study of a single subject or, in a minority of cases, of multi-disciplinary studies such as the humanities or expressive arts. The second was where courses combined both the academic and professional elements in what could be described as applied subject studies. In the case of the first approach, it was rare to find a curriculum method course designed for, and restricted to, students following a particular subject. Such students generally took a curriculum course common to all students, whatever their specialist subject, and these courses seldom offered differentiated work matched to the particular knowledge and experience of the students. In some institutions, more advanced curriculum courses in certain subjects were available as options, but there was a small number of others where students were not required to follow a curriculum course related in any way to their specialist subject. Main subject studies are considered in more detail later in this Chapter.

All institutions offered a range of curriculum courses designed to equip students as general class teachers responsible for teaching a broad curriculum. Such courses were focused on the acquisition of relevant knowledge, concepts and skills, and on the ways in which children's learning might be most effectively guided. The amount of time devoted to these curriculum courses in the BEd varied widely (see examples in Figure 5), but was seldom adequate. Institutions had chosen very different ways of allocating this time to the separate curriculum components. As remarked above, the majority of institutions offered a range of relatively short compulsory courses. Others concentrated on a compulsory core and allowed students to choose just two or three additional courses from a range of electives. Because of the low allocation of time overall given to this element of the course, nowhere was the tension between breadth and depth resolved satisfactorily. On the one hand, the attempt to provide insights into the whole primary curriculum resulted in unacceptably low time allocations for some of the individual compulsory components. On the other hand, where an option system operated, it sometimes had the effect of unduly narrowing the range of students' professional expertise. For example, in three institutions it meant that individual students missed one or more important areas of the curriculum such as science, environmental education or music. Another way of attempting to cover a broad curriculum within the time made available for curriculum courses was to group together certain subjects to form a broader area, for example humanities, but then to allocate the course less time than would have been required to offer each of the subjects separately. It was normal for humanities courses to contain history and geography, but there were variations in the other subjects they included. In four institutions history and geography were grouped with religious education, in two with science, and in one with literature and social studies. Three institutions did not make the humanities course compulsory but included it in an option system, with the result that some students did not encounter this area of the curriculum at all. Such groupings were often intended to give students experience of ways of working similar to those found in thematic and topic work in primary schools, but all too often this arrangement resulted in insufficient attention being paid to the individual subjects within the groupings.

Institutions attempted in a variety of ways to meet the needs of students training for different age groups. In most, though regrettably not all, curriculum courses some separate consideration was given to provision for the older and the younger children. The exceptions did not provide the students with a sufficiently precise focus.

In the BEd degree, the majority of the institutions offered a range of courses in mathematics, language, science, physical education, religious education, the humanities, and the creative and expressive arts. Of these, the courses in mathematics and language were compulsory in all cases. The contact time allocated to the former varied between 43 hours and 184 hours, with the majority lying between 80 and 110 hours. In practice many courses were unable to fulfil all that was expected of them, and only in the more substantial was it generally considered that students had adequate opportunities not only to consider a range of content but also to experience a variety of teaching and learning approaches, problem solving, and investigational work. The majority of tutors placed great importance on providing such a variety of experience. In a few cases optional courses allowed students to spend additional time on mathematics, but in general it appeared that such options were reserved for other curriculum areas. Most courses included some attention to number, measures, shape, graphical work, teaching aids and reviews of published textbooks. In addition, many course designs had recognised the limited mathematical knowledge and lack of confidence of many students and attempted to overcome these problems. In almost all the courses there was considerable emphasis on the language used by teachers and pupils and its influence on the quality of learning. Some courses also gave particular attention to the relationship between language work and mathematics. In contrast, links between mathematics and other aspects of the primary curriculum received little attention, though there were some good examples.

The average time allocation for language courses was 100 hours, and in the majority of instances the time was well distributed and the courses proceeded at a well-judged pace. Some institutions encouraged the students to top up their compulsory courses with language-related options, for instance on children's literature or on language development in the young child. In one college a complicated system of core study and options led to a wide disparity in the ground covered by individual students. In the curriculum language courses, the teaching of reading received particularly close attention. All the courses took a comprehensive view of the reading process as involving talking and listening, and as being related to writing. Tutors took care to point to the essentially eclectic nature of the teaching task and avoided a restrictively narrow concept of teaching reading. There was wider variation in the knowledge brought to bear on the development of other aspects of language ability, and some received insufficient expert attention to encourage the students to reassess preconceptions. Examples were the principal features of children's language development throughout the primary years, varieties of writing, and the organisation of texts, both spoken and written. The majority of courses provided students with insufficient help to understand clearly the place of English, or language, within the whole primary curriculum, that is to say how language ability should be developed in the context of the various elements of the curriculum and how in turn these can be more effectively learned by appropriate language activities. There was little evidence anywhere of the study of the structure of language.

The training of primary teachers: the primary school curriculum

Some institutions did not offer curriculum courses in all aspects of the primary curriculum. In some instances this was owing to a lack of qualified tutors, and in many institutions certain courses were sustained by a single tutor or by part-timers, as explained in Chapter 4. While many tutors coped well in these circumstances, others found the task difficult, particularly where part-time involvement precluded adequate discussion of course structure and the complex links between the various parts.

In view of the statutory place of religious education (RE) in the school curriculum, it is surprising that a small number of courses did not offer this subject at all. In one institution, only those who followed RE as a subject study had a curriculum course to equip them for work in school. In two others, there was no systematic preparation in the subject for intending primary teachers, while in a fourth there was none for junior-middle years teachers and a mere eight hours for infant teachers. Only about half the institutions were known to give all students over 20 hours of curriculum work in RE, and two of these allocated over 50 hours. One cause for concern was that, even where courses were adequate in length and breadth, the students' own understanding of the nature of religion was often insufficient for them to recognise ways in which RE could build upon everyday classroom activities such as reading stories and topic work. To counteract this, more emphasis is needed on building the students' understanding of religion at an adult level: its major concepts, its use of language, the fundamental questions it asks and the way various religions set about answering them, as well as training students to teach the subject. The paucity of good examples of RE in the primary schools where students gained their teaching practice was an additional cause for concern in several institutions.

BEd primary students were usually required to take a curriculum course in physical education (PE), for which the time allocation ranged from 24 to 90 hours. Almost all the courses incorporated gymnastics, dance, and games (which usually included athletics), and several added swimming. The majority of the time was wisely spent on practical work, in which the students experienced for themselves the nature and feeling of a variety of activities in PE and at the same time learned about its educational possibilities. In the best of the courses, observation-based study played an important part in teaching students how to assess children's performance and to recognise progression in PE. The students regularly worked in pairs and in groups and they studied their partner or others in action. Sometimes they looked for the effectiveness of a movement such as throwing, and at other times for qualities of movement in a dance task, or for versatility of response in gymnastics. Assessments were discusssed and reconsidered, often with the aid of further demonstrations and in response to suggestions and questions from tutors, and principles were drawn out where time allowed. In the more substantial courses it was possible for students to acquire at least a provisional capacity to observe accurately, perceptively, and with insights based upon knowledge. They developed some competence in analysing their own and children's movements, using techniques which they had developed during the course. Their observations enabled them to discuss the issues of competition and sharing in different forms of physical education activity.

Curriculum studies are particularly demanding of time if a broad curriculum is to be covered to any satisfactory depth. As has been indicated above, there were marked differences from one institution to another in the amount of contact time allocated to the various elements of the primary curriculum, and this varied from as little as 4 hours to over 90 hours. In one institution only 15 hours were allocated to a course divided equally between geography and history and described as environmental studies. Another environmental studies course provided just 18 hours for science and 12 hours for geography. In a third institution, 15 hours of inter-disciplinary study resulted in barely three hours of history. Pressure of time often affected the way in which the courses were taught, leading often to direct delivery by the tutor, and inadequate practical work and student participation. There can be little value in a curriculum course of less than 30 hours' duration, even for students who bring to it a sound knowledge of the subject, and some need considerably more than this. Many curriculum courses in the BEd undoubtedly made inadequate provision for students' future needs.

Problems of coverage and pressures on time were even more acute in the PGCE. In three institutions, for example, the allocation for RE ranged from 4.5 to 12 hours, and nowhere did PE courses exceed 30 hours. In four institutions it was possible for students to complete their PGCE course without any work at all in humanities, and in those that did include it as a compulsory component the time allocation ranged from 4 to 48 hours. Courses which largely focused on immediate practical needs left little room for deeper study and the acquisition of enough understanding to deal with pupils' second order questions, or to assist long-term planning of work. Such courses were characterised by a rapid pace consistent with their brevity, and very few involved contact with children.

In language and mathematics the courses in a small number of institutions were particularly short: for example, 24 hours for mathematics and 40 hours for language. In both cases the time was inadequate for students to gain confidence in the subject area; it was sufficient to gain only a fleeting contact with fundamental issues. Institutions recognised that primary school teachers need to understand a number of important language issues, but all too often the limited time allocation made it difficult to fit these in. It was to the credit of the tutors responsible that most institutions managed, through a skilful combination of contact time and school experience, to introduce students to the areas of greatest importance. In addition, some managed a deeper study of language development or children's literature in which the theoretical and practical elements were well combined. Most purported to deal with the assessment of language and its relationship to teaching, but there was a tendency to concentrate on narrow or shallow aspects of standardised tests and the marking of children's written work. Few addressed systematically the monitoring of progress through a range of strategies based upon a firm understanding of language itself, how it works, and its development in children.

In mathematics courses the broad structure was often similar to the comparable BEd courses but the time constraint was much sharper. The difficulties this created were compounded by the fact that few of the graduates entering primary training had taken mathematics as part of their undergraduate studies, and many had not studied any mathematics since O-level/CSE, thus having had five or more years without studying the subject. Bearing in mind this long gap, the courses needed to give the students confidence and competence in mathematics, a positive attitude towards the subject, and the skills to teach it effectively in primary schools. Frequently, however, the shorter courses were inadequate and of little substance. Important topics such as assessment or meeting individual needs were often covered in single lectures, if at all. Only one college offered an option course in addition to the compulsory mathematics component. This course of 96 hours was for middle school students and was carefully planned to extend the range, content, and depth of study of the compulsory course, of which it was twice the length.

As noted above, in the shorter curriculum courses, both in BEd and in PGCE courses, there was a marked tendency for tutors to dominate proceedings; these courses were typified by a dearth of practical work and the likelihood that students would not be involved with children either on the college premises or through school visits. A particular challenge for the providers of curriculum courses is the need to develop students' understanding of a relevant subject as well as training them to teach it. This is particularly difficult for those students who ceased to study a particular subject at the age of 14. For example, in a well resourced session on electrical circuits, many students demonstrated a lack of everyday knowledge such as the voltage of ordinary single cell batteries. Similarly, a weakness in background knowledge on the part of some students was evident in a practical music-making session which involved the use of BBC radio programmes and a discussion of tonic sol-fa. An attempt to overcome this kind of difficulty was made in a college where a two-part professional course was provided, initially dealing with the nature of the subject then proceeding to its professional application. This clear separation of the academic from the professional was not wholly satisfactory because it took too little account of the range of students' knowledge and their levels of understanding, but tutors were engaged in devising means to take more account of individual differences. This tension between tackling content and gaining an adequate understanding of the teaching and learning processes was present in most subject areas but it was often particularly acute in science. In one institution, for example, the available time was filled by attention to scientific processes and skills and to preparaton for teaching practice. Scant attention was paid to relevant knowledge and concepts, and the students were left unsure about how to select and develop subject matter in a progressive way.

In the expressive arts courses, in BEd and PGCE alike, most curriculum courses demonstrated relevance to the students' future needs and to the practicalities of the classroom, but the acquisition of experience and the development of appropriate skills also usually required more time than was allowed. For example, art topics included the display of work in the classroom, the illustration of themes using shape, line, colour and texture, and discussion of the relationship between visual and spoken language. There were similar examples in other areas of the curriculum of good use of limited time. Physical education sessions included the handling and care of apparatus, and in music the students considered the role of the subject in children's games.

Students were frequently asked to relate course work to their school experience and this acted as a powerful aid to understanding. For example, in a session concerned with ways of developing and extending reading skills, a group of BEd fourth year students drew upon practical work in reading which they had carried out in a junior school. The quality and depth of discussion achieved were due in no small measure to the group's ability to draw upon these experiences and to relate them to issues such as children's reading interests, the evaluation of spoken language, and the effective matching of reading material to the needs of the reader. The students also benefited from opportunities and encouragement to apply what they had learned in curriculum studies to their experience in schools, where they spent half a day each week planning and organising a number of group activities for a class of juniors. Students were seen working with three groups of children, two of which were making clay plaques using a live tortoise for inspiration, while a third worked outside drawing and painting pictures of trees. The students helped the children sensitively, supporting and guiding them in their work through a subtle blend of suggestions, comments and questions. The opportunity to put into practice principles and ideas already discussed during the course helped the students to develop confidence in the planning, development, and evaluation of the children's work.

There were many excellent examples of institutions which included work with children as an integral part of curriculum courses. Schools were visited and children came to the college premises. The value of such an interplay between the taught course and its classroom application was exemplified in a language session where students worked in college with a class of 26 infant children. Prior to this the students had assessed, during their time in the school, the children's strengths and weaknesses as readers and they subsequently devised a range of games and other activities addressed to these identified needs for use during the college session. The students derived considerable benefit from working closely with the children; in particular they gained a valuable and a practical insight into the needs and development of individuals. This kind of direct involvement was usefully supplemented in a number of courses by the use of video tapes which showed children at work; other courses used samples of children's work to broaden students' experience. Carefully planned experience sharpened the professional focus of the courses and often enhanced the quality of the work. Constraints upon time, and to some extent finance, limited the extent to which work with children could be included in curriculum courses. A minority of colleges did not identify it as a priority and as a result their students missed potentially valuable experience.

Many PGCE courses provided good examples of the way in which curriculum courses can be related to practical experience in schools. In a number of institutions effective links were developed between the theory and practice of teaching through the use of school-focused assignments. The setting of appropriate assignments at suitable points in the course provided a useful context for drawing together a number of different strands, both professional and academic. In one, all the themes of the course were closely integrated with the students' assignments. Assessment was based on a journal which students kept throughout the course and submitted to their tutors at intervals. The first assignment was on analysis of first hand experience in schools early in the course; the second related to the theme of individual differences. These were followed by an analysis of the first teaching practice and an exercise related to the second theme of creativity and motivation. Assessment was completed by a report on team teaching in school and work relating to the final course theme of current educational issues. In another example, the first term's work was assessed by an essay which required a theoretical and a school-based section. In the second term assessment was by means of an individual study folder.

As far as the available time permitted, most curriculum courses gave attention to both short- and long-term objectives in planning work for children.

Some of the work was focused quite precisely on provision for children of a particular age group. For example, in one effective science session the students discussed weather records made in school by a reception class. Together, the tutor and students addressed such issues as the provision of appropriate activities for the youngest children, and how these might be developed and taken further with older children in the infant school. Similarly, in a history session with a group of second year students, a tape/slide presentation was used to illustrate the wide range of primary source material which is available. A subsequent visit to a nearby castle was used as a starting point for considering the selection and use of historical resource materials in upper junior classes.

A number of courses were specifically aimed at preparing students for work with younger children. Several mathematics courses were particularly well related to the infant age group. In one session, for example, a group of third year students discussed and evaluated computer games for infants, then devised their own games and activities for children using a variety of computers. Not all courses were equally successful. In one science course provided for early years students, some of the themes were not effectively adapted to show what is appropriate for children in infant classes; too little attention was given to the science which children can learn from everyday activities in the infant school, such as cooking, the use of constructional toys, and exploring the properties of sand and water.

Many curriculum courses which ostensibly provided for the full primary age range paid too little attention to age differences and in particular to the youngest children. Typically, an interesting environmental education session on rural and urban fieldwork, provided for a mixed infant/junior group, had little relevance for those who wished to teach the youngest children. A potentially valuable mathematics session on obtaining data and its graphical representation related only indirectly to the early years. It is clear that many courses would benefit from a sharper focus on particular age groups.

Curriculum courses tended to be self-contained, and references were rarely made to related work which the students had covered in other aspects of the BEd or PGCE courses, or to work on the curriculum as a whole. The students were usually left to make the connections for themselves. One exception was seen in a science session on electrical circuitry where a useful link was established with the binary system in mathematics by students who were working out a sequence of flashing lights. Another example, in an RE session, involved a review of children's literature in an effort to identify its potential for raising religious and moral issues. The benefits of team teaching for the development of such links were demonstrated when a mathematics and an education tutor jointly taught the topic of early number work. Not only did the session deal with processes such as sorting, discriminating and classifying, but close attention was also paid to the nature of number and to children's conceptual development.

In a small number of institutions the tutors made positive efforts to link curriculum elements and other strands of the course. In one institution particular tutors taught both the academic and professional aspects of a subject. By this means science, for example, was systematically related to the curriculum as a whole, and in particular to mathematics, art, and language, by tutors who taught both education studies and science. In another institution, tutors shared a common approach to a number of important issues, including provision for the range of individual differences found in ordinary classes. In a third, a distinct and clearly articulated philosophy provided one of the means by which students developed a coherent understanding of primary school work. In general, however, too little attention was paid to cross-curricular issues and, in most institutions, links between various parts of the courses remained tenuous. Those teaching different parts of the courses had not achieved a common appreciation and approach to cross-curricular issues, such as provision for individual differences, assessment, and evaluation. Their teaching was not informed by an appreciation of what the students would have gathered from other parts of the courses. There was, however, a much more secure relationship between curriculum courses and school experience, and at its best this promoted a rounded view of the demands of classroom teaching. An example is provided by an institution where the students spent a morning a week teaching small groups of pupils while an associated mathematics curriculum course considered broader issues of discipline, match and motivation along with the teaching of mathematics. In the least satisfactory situations there was little evidence that course planning was a collective endeavour, and links between college work and school experience were minimal.

Where time for the curriculum courses was adequate, the content of most of the sessions was well chosen and the sessions themselves were well prepared and taught. Most involved a degree of active learning on the students' part, and many tutors provided good models for the students' own practice. Much of the work was well resourced and the tutors' use of audio-visual aids and other facilities was generally commendable. However, the value of a small number of sessions was limited by the choice of content. In some cases key ideas were omitted while in others the orientation had little relevance for intending primary teachers. Sometimes the teaching approaches failed to exploit potentially valuable content. There were wide variations in the extent to which content was related to specific age groups and there was a tendency to overlook provision for individual differences, in particular the needs of the youngest children. Some institutions demonstrated particular strength in the early years, but they were not numerous.

As indicated earlier a few institutions provided curriculum courses which were additional to the broad range of curriculum courses taken by all students. These courses were most often available as options for those who wished to develop a particular curricular strength. Two examples serve to illustrate the extent to which these courses were potentially valuable. At one institution, main subject studies in both history and geography were complemented by a compulsory basic curriculum course in environmental studies. While the main geography students had no further course open to them, the historians could take a substantial additional curriculum option entitled 'history in the landscape'. This combination of main subject studies, the compulsory course in environmental studies, and the additional curriculum option constituted a good preparation for class teaching and gave the students a curricular strength in history. The geographers lacked this opportunity for further study in depth. In another institution, all the geographers followed a rigorous subject studies course and a multi-disciplinary curriculum course entitled 'investigation techniques'. These students were strongly encouraged to take an option course in the teaching of the subject. For those who followed this route, the combination of studies was an effective way of enabling them to gain a curricular strength.

Most of the additional curriculum courses linked to main subject studies were particularly relevant to students' future professional needs. They covered such areas as curriculum planning, the acquisition by children of appropriate concepts and skills, fieldwork, assessment, and the use of resources. At their best they were of considerable interest and presented the students with intellectual challenge. For example, one course for geographers involved a study of rural settlements, contrasting the development of farms, examining rural settlement patterns and using activities such as 'nearest neighbour analysis'. The teaching and learning approaches employed were suitable for use in schools.

The additional curriculum courses were generally taught by tutors who were also responsible for the main subject study, enabling each aspect to build upon the other. Where this was not the case there was some evidence that course content was unnecessarily repeated and that insufficient challenge was offered. These problems indicate the need to ensure good liaison if different tutors are to be responsible for the two aspects. These additional courses were of a satisfactory standard and complemented the main academic studies well. Almost all of them offered adequate preparation for general class teaching and many prepared students to offer a curricular strength. A few main subject courses included elements of pedagogy which were both academically rigorous and of practical value to the intending primary teacher. Several mathematics courses offered particularly good examples of this kind. Students who followed such courses along with the common curriculum course were receiving a sound preparation for class teaching.

There were few instances where PGCE students built on their previous degrees by taking special courses designed to apply their specialist knowledge to the needs of primary school children. As with main subject students on BEd degrees, the majority of graduates followed the common curriculum courses which were taken by all their peers. On occasions, however, graduates drew enterprisingly upon their degree studies in their own assignments. In one case, a study of the docks benefited from a student's geographical strengths, while in another the student's knowledge of biology proved invaluable in preparing material on the life cycle of the whale. A few institutions attempted to build on PGCE students' degree studies by allocating up to a third of the total contact time to the study of a single subject or to a multi-disciplinary study such as environmental studies. This high level of emphasis usually enabled the students to offer a curriculum strength in their subject but weakened their capacity to contribute across the full primary curriculum. As most will eventually take on the role of general class teacher, this over-emphasis upon a specialist contribution within the constraints of a one-year course failed to meet the broad needs of primary school teachers. In sum, most of the PGCE courses were found to be equipping able students to cope as class teachers despite curriculum courses which received a very small time allocation. This was because a number of the better courses engendered confidence through well organised, sustained contact with schools. Very few prepared students to contribute a curricular strength.

Up to this point attention has been concentrated largely upon the general features of curriculum courses. Two specific examples have been selected to provide greater detail and to illustrate the opportunities, constraints, and achievements to be found within these courses. These examples, which describe and assess how BEd and PGCE students were acquiring competence in the teaching of science and the expressive arts, are given in Appendix 2 to the report.

Specialist subject studies

Earlier in this section is the description of the ways in which institutions provided intending primary teachers with specialist subject study in BEd, in the form either of a single subject or of a grouping of two or more subjects. The majority of BEd specialist subject courses were not designed to relate directly to students' future careers as primary teachers, and their content was not selected with professional application in view. Their content and general style were similar to those found in other higher education courses, and the students were commonly taught alongside students working for other degrees.

Institutions varied in the emphasis they gave to the students' mastery of the subject or area of learning at their own level and its professional relevance, and there were many reasons for this. These included the attitudes of validating bodies; whether the courses were jointly taught with DipHE, BA, or BSc students; and the experience and interests of the tutors. Some institutions saw subject studies as making an important contribution to the personal education of students. They held the view that if students are to master a subject or an area of learning they need to study the distinctive nature of their subjects, and the essential concepts, associated knowledge, skills, and characteristic ways of reasoning and working. They therefore focused firmly upon academic standards and built upon the research experience of tutors. Other institutions sought to combine such academic rigour with professional relevance. There were differences even within institutions; for example, an academically demanding yet professionally relevant main subject study entitled Mathematics in Education was offered alongside an equally rigorous geography course which concentrated on developing the students' own mastery of the subject.

A significant factor in the level of attainment reached by students in their subject studies courses was the time allocation. There were wide variations, from almost 600 hours to as few as 135 hours, with most institutions providing about 350 hours in three year courses and 420 hours in four year courses. Most of the main subject studies offered in the BEd courses matched areas of learning found in the primary school, but a number of institutions continued to offer subjects which are not reflected in the primary school curriculum, such as business studies and psychology.

Another factor which limited the students' level of achievement in specialist subject studies was the modest A-level qualifications of some of those admitted to certain courses. For example, in one mathematics course the qualifications of the first year students ranged from grade C at O-level to grade A at A-level. In multi-disciplinary courses it was rare to find students who were suitably qualified in each of the constituent elements. In creative arts courses, for example, very few students had an A-level or its equivalent in music where this was one of the constituents. It was not unusual for the A-level qualifications of BEd students to be rather weaker than those of their fellows following the same elements of the course but aiming for other degrees. As a consequence, BEd students often struggled to cope in the early stages. The demands made upon students in their specialist subject studies varied considerably, to the extent that in some instances the expectations were unrealistically high while in others the students were not fully extended. Some courses accepted students with a wide range of O and A-level backgrounds, with the result that the work was sometimes at too low a level for those students who already had a good grasp of fundamentals.

The substantial majority of tutors responsible for specialist subject courses had good academic qualifications, most with research experience which brought both substance and added interest to their teaching. In most instances they adopted a good range of teaching styles, and audio-visual aids, primary source materials, practical work and first hand experience were all used to good effect. There were some good examples of formal lectures, dealing with such topics as a consideration of the moral and religious themes in 'Middlemarch' and the solution of inequalities by algebraic and graphical methods. These main subject studies were for the most part intellectually challenging and were appreciated by the students, with very few teaching sessions falling below an acceptable standard. A minority of tutors adopted an unduly expository style, which led to a predominance of note taking, and made possible few opportunities for discussion and the development of reasoning. This teaching approach insufficiently challenged the most able students and was, on occasions, unhelpful to those who were experiencing difficulties or were less well prepared owing to a lack of previous study. In many cases the students had done too little reading in preparation for lectures and seminars. This affected their ability to contribute to the taught sessions, and to gain maximum benefit from them.

Quality in schools: the initial training of teachers

Inadequate preparation by students was often a consequence of the many competing demands made upon them by the range of courses being studied at any given time. Except in the fourth year, students were usually following education studies and several curriculum courses at the same time as main subject studies. Preparation for, and follow up of, school experience made further inroads into the time for study and reflection.

As noted earlier, the content of most specialist subject courses was similar to that experienced by students working for other degrees. Quite apart from fulfilling its function as a course of higher education at an appropriate level, this was sometimes of direct relevance to teaching in the primary school. Examples of such relevance were the use of first hand sources in history and of pond-dipping techniques in science. There were other instances, however, where the choice of content was somewhat limited in the extent to which it could support the teacher in his or her task. For example, the majority of science students studied biological science and lacked a secure foundation in physical science; half the history courses contained little or no world history and two-thirds did not cover local history; and a third of the religious studies courses were too narrow in scope.

In some cases, elements were deliberately incorporated in the course because they were potentially useful for teachers as well as important for the study of the subject in its own right. This applied in science, where the emphasis on practical work and direct experience had relevance for the students' own practice in schools, and where, for example, the study of the plant and animal kingdoms which featured in most courses acted as a resource for the future. There were instances where students were helped to consider how work done at their own level could be adapted for use with children. For example, in a history session with first year BEd students, during a study of vernacular architecture in the built environment, the tutor gave an illustrated talk which focused on timber framed buildings. Students compared the various styles and discussed fieldwork in which they had sketched houses, drawn plans, and made notes about building materials. Concepts and skills used in fieldwork were listed and the group considered ways of developing this approach with children. In some cases, tutors simply drew attention to the relevance of certain subject matter. In an interesting, though uncommon initiative, one institution which offered a joint BA/BEd main subject course in history programmed a separate series of seminars for intending teachers, enabling them to consider the application of the subject to the primary classroom. This device deserved wider currency, and it was disappointing to find that, when planning curriculum courses, institutions had commonly taken little account of the content covered in specialist subject studies.

A small number of institutions offered subject studies courses which combined academic content with professional applications to the primary school classroom, and in some instances this combination worked well. For example, in a session on Krishna myths and associated festivals, students learned about the cultural significance of drama and adapted a story for dramatic performance in schools. There were variations in quality even within individual institutions. For example, a group of geography students followed a series of particularly demanding lectures on soil structures in the British Isles; they subsequently collected and analysed soil from a variety of locations and at the same time considered how this academic knowledge and these ways of working might be useful in a primary school. In marked contrast, another group in the same institution spent a full afternoon on the subject of coal, in which a poorly prepared lecture was illustrated by a number of uninspiring posters which showed the location of coalfields, the layout of a mine and methods of extraction. There was a desultory discussion about the formation of coal and its uses, with little helpful comment on how the topic might be taught in school. Some of the courses were of a particularly high standard, illustrating the rich potential of this approach, but the difficulties of achieving both academic credibility and professional relevance within the same course were all too often evidenced by the work seen.

6 The training of primary teachers: professional and classroom skills

Teaching approaches

All the institutions provided opportunities for the students to experience and to reflect upon the different teaching approaches used in primary schools. Mainly, these were dealt with in curriculum courses and in professional and education studies, and practised during school experience. The effectiveness of the training was often linked to the way in which the students themselves were taught and to the tutor's ability to relate the students' experience directly to children's learning. In approximately half the institutions, there were examples of work in several curricular areas where the teaching was appropriate for adults and also exemplified ways in which the work could be approached with children. For example, in a science curriculum course students who knew very little about structure and forces were asked to build, out of newpaper, structures which would hold a given weight at a height of one metre from the floor. As they worked the tutor helped them to understand the scientific knowledge and concepts involved and to identify processes and skills which they were using. The group then discussed how a similar approach could be used in schools. In another example, the students came to a curriculum language course well prepared to discuss the use of reading schemes. Most gave a clear and critical presentation of the material they had looked at and the tutors asked questions and offered comments. A number of substantial points emerged about the benefits and drawbacks of particular reading schemes and of reading schemes in general. There was a relaxed and business-like atmosphere and much was achieved. In an earlier session the students had listened to a lecture on approaches to teaching reading and then discussed practical steps they had taken during a series of half days of school experience. In a music curriculum course the tutor introduced two new songs suitable for young children and illustrated possible approaches to teaching them, using a tape recording, piano accompaniment, guitar accompaniment, and the voice plus actions. As the students learned the songs they were also asked to comment on each teaching approach in terms of appropriateness and purpose. They were then asked about the value of the songs and what the children would learn from them. Technical language was introduced as appropriate and the tutor's approach was a model in giving encouragement and praise.

In contrast to these examples of good practice, there were occasions when too little attention was given to teaching approaches and the students lacked practical and realistic advice about classroom organisation. For example in a science curriculum course for PGCE students, 24 different commercially-produced assignment cards together with associated materials for practical work were set out for sampling. Other relevant published material was also on display. The students moved round the materials either individually or in groups in order to identify possibilities for the infant age range. The assignment cards, which were produced for older primary children, were to be used as sources of ideas. The tutor worked with individuals and responded to questions. This session merely provided ideas for activities. The inexperienced students found it very difficult to adapt the ideas suggested on the assignments cards for use with younger children, there was little attempt to relate the work to children's progressive development of concepts, knowledge and skills, and there was no systematic consideration of how the work might be presented and organised with a class of infants. There was considerable variation between institutions, and between curriculum courses within institutions, in the extent to which students were taught to use a wide variety of teaching approaches within each area of the school curriculum. In the most successful institutions, this was achieved in a significant proportion of curricular areas.

Almost all education studies courses referred to research into teaching styles but too often this was at a descriptive level and its application to teaching various types of material to children of particular ages was seldom examined critically. Nevertheless, there were some examples of activities which helped the students to relate their understanding of teaching approaches to work in schools. In one education studies seminar, students who had been making video recordings of one another's teaching in schools practised methods of analysing teaching approaches as they watched a video recording of an experienced teacher telling a fairy story to a class of six year olds. In another institution, second year students completed written assignments linking research findings on teaching styles with their own classroom experience. In one college, second year BEd students were given a lecture on ways in which two contrasting psychological theories of learning had been applied in the development of a number of structured and commercially produced teaching programmes, some of them computer based: for the following week's session arrangements were made for pupils who had been using one of the programmes to discuss their experience of it with the students.

All courses recognised that students need practical experience in schools to try out the teaching approaches which they have been taught. The majority of students on block teaching practices were placed in schools and in classrooms where they could do this, and the results were often encouraging. An example of such activity was where students set out to base their work on children's first hand experience. Some of the students were particularly venturesome and innovative, either in devising the content of their work or in introducing new organisational procedures for which they could provide sound and well-considered reasons.

Conversely, a number of students found themselves in schools where teaching approaches differed from those advocated by the training institution. In these cases the students tended to conform to the schools' methods rather than those suggested by their tutors. This tension occurred in a number of cases. In one example, it was noted that the tutors were training the students to use newer approaches while many of the schools being used for teaching practice were committed to more traditional approaches. Although the majority of students seen on teaching practices were able to try out their own ideas there were a few instances where students were unhappy about the dichotomy between the college's expectations and what the schools required them to do. The implications are clear for the selection of teaching practice schools; there is a need for the tutors to negotiate the students' programmes with the teachers concerned.

Much useful practice was gained by students working with small groups of children, particularly in the early stages of training, since this reduced the organisational demands made by full classes and allowed the students to concentrate on the children's response to their teaching. In some institutions the best of this group work took place during block teaching practices but for the majority it occurred when the students were attached to schools for a half or a full day each week. On these serial practices there was often a group of up to 12 students in a school and this allowed the tutors to work more closely with them than was possible on block practices where the students were more widely distributed. In one example, six students worked with small groups of children on art and craft activities which included collage and model making. Each student unobtrusively observed one child in particular and made tape recordings and notes of the child's responses. These were compared and discussed when the students met their tutor in college. Sometimes students worked in pairs, and often the size and composition of the group of children were varied according to the activity to be undertaken. For example, in one college the PGCE students were attached to schools for a day a week during the autumn term, and one of their assignments was to practise reading stories. Once they had got to know the children, they selected stories from the school and college libraries and discussed their choices with the class teacher, tutor and other students. Two students would sit with the children so that while one read the other could observe the reader and the children. Later the students compared their impressions of the readers' presentation and the children's responses. When the students met with the tutor and class teachers for discussions at the end of the day general points were drawn out; for example, ways of seating the children so that all could be seen by a quick glance from the reader, the use of the eyes to make contact with all listeners, and ways of handling interruptions. Such profitable experiences in trying out teaching approaches applied in about half the curriculum courses. Less valuable experiences were also in evidence; for example, where the content of the work was undemanding and the children were consequently inattentive, where the students ran out of material before the end of the lesson, and where the children were given too little stimulus through the choice of materials or the students' use of language.

Only a minority of institutions emphasised sufficiently the importance of providing an environment in school designed to stimulate the children's interests and to act as a resource for learning. Some schools encouraged students to create such a learning environment but others gave the question little attention. More institutions could ask schools to help students with display, and some should feature it more prominently in the taught course. The provision of primary bases in some institutions encouraged and gave a focus to these ideas, but they are capable of being realised in those which do not have such facilities.

There are some teaching approaches and skills which are particularly important for working with the youngest children in school, i.e. in the age range 3 to 8 years. These include, for example, organising play activities, and the ability to extend and enrich the children's spontaneous activities and guide their learning. Some institutions helped students to develop these skills by a strong emphasis on observing young children's development and behaviour in the course of school-based work. However, it was much more common to find that the emphasis was on approaches which were interesting and appropriate for older primary children but less suitable for the younger children. There was evidence that too little attention was paid in the majority of the institutions to provision for these children. This could often be traced to the lack of staff who were experienced in working with the youngest children and who could teach students how to use appropriate activities to develop, for example, the beginnings of mathematics, language, early ideas of time and space, social awareness and manual skills.

Institutions generally provided instruction in the use of audio-visual aids, ranging from the blackboard to television, and in the operation of reprographic devices widely used in schools. This instruction was usually offered in the form of a short course which taught the students how to use such aids and demonstrated examples of commercially produced material such as film strips, wall charts, and tape recordings. Advice on the selection and use of audio-visual material to support teaching in particular subjects was sometimes given in curriculum courses; for example, students in a BEd curriculum course in science viewed a radio-vision programme and then discussed its potential as a starting point for work in schools.

Most institutions also provided a computer familiarisation course as part of initial training. Although a few of these courses were substantial, most were short, averaging about 20 hours. In their nature and scope these were similar to those provided for intending secondary teachers, and the fuller account of the use of microcomputers given in Chapter 7 applies with equal force to the training of primary teachers. The examples described there could be replicated here, and the general conclusion applies to both phases of training. The computer courses were self-contained, and the application of computers and other forms of electronic technology elsewhere in the students' training was rare.

The majority of tutors offered good models for the students' future work in schools. Many skilfully employed a variety of approaches and techniques, some of which are referred to earlier in this chapter. Much of the best teaching demonstrated the importance of good planning and preparation, suitability of content, and the use of a variety of well-chosen activities. It was conducted at a suitable pace, encouraged active participation from the students, and made skilled use of audio-visual and other resources. The teaching was less than satisfactory in only a small minority of the sessions observed; for example where the students were spoon-fed or the tutor attempted to cover too much ground. At worst, the methods used relied excessively on direct teaching, as in one PGCE curriculum course in mathematics where the tutor, because of shortage of time, used expository methods which gave the students few opportunities for them to find out or to think for themselves. Students in such situations were encouraged in passivity and were at risk of seeing teaching as simply a process of handing out parcels of unexamined knowledge. There were many examples of work in small groups, but only a few institutions provided differentiated work within the groups to take account of the different levels of subject knowledge which students brought to the course. This matter deserves further consideration, since students may well base their group work with children on models of this kind.

Planning

In most cases the students' first experience of planning work for children occurred in connection with school attachments when they began to teach individuals, small groups, and occasionally a whole class. This planning was usually concerned with the preparation of single lessons, often based on work which the students were doing in curriculum courses. The students usually discussed the lesson content and presentation with their curriculum course tutor and prepared a lesson plan which was generally based on the pattern adopted by the institution for teaching practice notes. After each school visit there was usually some follow-up discussion and preparation for the next session. For example, BEd nursery students studying creative activities in nursery schools discussed practical work carried out on serial school visits. They recounted observations of children playing with water and with dough, and the tutor helped them to consider ways of extending these learning activities through the use of additional materials and tools, and by appropriate teacher intervention. Children's developmental stages were outlined and were related to their responses to the materials to help the students understand the teacher's role in planning for the children's progressive development through play. The tutor examined practical and organisational aspects of such work and drew out the educational objectives of creative activities. It was planned that on the next school visit the students would introduce finger painting. They practised the techniques and discussed ways of presenting, organising and developing the activity.

At times a group of students planned, with their tutor and the class teacher, a piece of work for a whole class. For example, six first year BEd students working with a fourth year class of 32 pupils in an 8 to 12 middle school were given the task of producing a play based on the story of Rama and Sita associated with the Hindu festival of Diwali. In the preparation period the tutor acted as a consultant while the students planned the work as a group and visited the college library and resource centre for material to supplement the resources provided by the school. The students decided to use a booklet produced by the school as the main script and to add dance and mime with masks and costume. During the morning they produced some superb masks on card for the children to use as models for their own work in the afternoon and worked out the casting of the play and the actions of the characters involved. Considering the inexperience of the students concerned they all showed great maturity and seriousness of purpose. All rose to the challenge of being given real responsibility for carrying out a practical activity within a limited period of time. It was very much a student-led activity, with the tutor giving encouragement and advice. In school the students followed their plan. The pupils' tasks were clearly explained and parts were given out. One student read through the script with the narrator, and the children were soon absorbed in making masks. Later, the sequence of actions was worked out with the accompaniment of tape-recorded Indian music. A few problems arose which had not been anticipated, such as how to interest the majority of children while the principal characters were on stage. These were considered at the follow-up session and noted as points to watch when drawing up plans in the future.

In ways such as these, students became increasingly familiar with the elements which need to be considered in devising individual lessons and with ways of setting out lesson plans. The introduction of lesson planning in connection with school experience was valuable since it was much more realistic than planning exercises carried out in the abstract for a notional class, and there was immediate feedback showing the strengths and weaknesses. Since the students worked as a group they were able to support one another and, where two or more shared a class, to offer sympathetic yet critical comment on the outcomes. Tutors who worked alongside the students in school occasionally set the students' planning into the wider context of the planning done by the class teacher and by the school as a whole.

For block teaching practices students prepared schemes of work for the whole period, which might vary in length from three or four weeks to practically a full term. Individual lessons were prepared within this framework and the students were briefed on the format to adopt for writing schemes of work and lesson plans. In virtually all cases the students made a preliminary visit to their teaching practice schools to gather information upon which to base their planning. Time and opportunities were generally available for the students to consult tutors about the preparation of schemes of work and individual lessons. There were examples of students being well supported during this period. In one, detailed attention was given to producing schemes of work and lesson plans, and essential features were fully discussed. The tutors guided students in devising plans for individual pupils, groups and the class. When preparing lessons the students were asked to consider learning intentions, content, strategy, organisation and resources. The tutors also gave the students useful advice on the evaluation of their teaching. Despite such good examples the picture, overall, was one of considerable variation between institutions in the amount and quality of help given to students in planning work for block teaching practices (see Chapter 8), and this was reflected in the quality of planning revealed by the students' teaching practice notebooks.

The planning of lessons and schemes of work in particular subject areas, and sometimes in multi-disciplinary areas, was usually studied in curriculum courses. In general the students were competent in devising lessons and units of work in subjects where they had undertaken a substantial curriculum course and where principles were linked to school experience. Thus, most students were able to plan and to execute work in language and mathematics. It was frequently the case in these two subjects that the curriculum courses were substantial, that the students had planned work for use in serial school practice and on several block teaching practices, and that this had been thoughtfully considered in follow-up sessions. Only a minority of institutions covered every aspect of the primary curriculum in sufficient depth to enable students to plan effectively in all of them. In the majority of cases some subjects were covered well while others received little more than token attention. Consequently, it was commonly the case that the students were able to plan effectively in some areas of the primary school curriculum but experienced difficulty with others. In some cases the students' difficulties arose from a limited grasp of subject matter and a consequent inability to select and use content for the progressive development of knowledge, concepts and skills, and to adapt it for the full ability range.

In all institutions education studies included aspects of curriculum planning such as aims and objectives and patterns of curriculum analysis and development. The topic was presented in a variety of ways in different institutions. In some, the principles were discussed and carefully related to the students' experience in schools, so that their relevance to lesson preparation and to curricular issues which the students had met in schools was demonstrated. An example was a lecture to third year BEd students which provided a clear outline of a commercially produced package designed to help teachers make use of specific objectives in planning work for less able children in ordinary schools. A sample set of checklists was placed on reserve in the college library, for students to consult, and follow-up seminars required students to improve and refine objectives which had been inadequately framed. Contrasting examples included a PGCE lecture where the history of curriculum theory was presented in an abstract and unimaginative way, relying on out-of-date analyses and with little to stimulate or assist the students professionally.

At its best, such work in education studies helped students in their preparation for school experience, familiarised them with current debate on curricular issues, and gave them perspectives on the curriculum as a whole. This broader view was supported by some of the curriculum courses which examined the place of the subject within the curriculum as a whole and its links with other areas of the school's work, but these matters were seldom given sufficient attention.

Towards the end of their course most students were able to plan, with the help of tutors and teachers, a well conceived outline of work to cover the period of a block teaching practice. This was usually expected of them for their final teaching practice. The majority were able to plan single lessons and topic or thematic work spread across a number of sessions. They were generally able to select appropriate content, resources, and teaching approaches for the group they were teaching. Yet it was exceptional to find students whose planning paid sufficiently close attention to the progressive development of knowledge, concepts, skills and attitudes. Most students, even in their final year, were less confident about long-term planning and in their perception of the curriculum as a whole. These are aspects which develop with experience and greater maturity. New teachers need further help with them as part of their induction into their first teaching post, but training institutions could do more by way of preparation. For example, there should be constant emphasis on the relationship between the whole curriculum and the various parts covered separately in curriculum courses and these should be linked to work in education studies.

Assessment

To varying extents, students were introduced to ways of assessing children's attainments to enable them to match the work to the children's capabilities and also to provide summative assessments of their performance. These included something about informal means of assessment, such as observing children at work, asking questions, and listening to children's explanations of how they came to a particular conclusion, and some knowledge of more formal procedures including tests commonly used in schools. Attention was sometimes given to aspects of assessment in education studies, usually as a distinct topic and often in components covering child development, individual differences and special needs. It was also included in some curriculum courses and occasionally in main subject studies.

Direct teaching about assessment in education studies, where it occurred, was concerned with aspects such as observational methods of assessing children's attainments, analysing examples of their work, the use of standardised tests, and the recording of children's progress. The work on observational methods was enhanced when opportunities were provided through school experience for the students to apply the principles and to practise the skills they had been studying. Work on standardised tests tended to be introduced at a descriptive and practical level rather than through a detailed consideration of underlying theory and statistical measures. This was appropriate given the complexity of ideas involved and the limited time available. For example, PGCE students were shown tests of creativity which they then performed themselves, and the tutor drew on this experience to discuss the mental processes which are sampled by such instruments. In another case, BEd students examined tests of spatial abilities, used them in schools, and discussed the results. Sometimes students had opportunities to extend this introductory work. For example, a lecture to fourth year BEd students studying methods of educational enquiry included work on standard deviation, the concept of statistical significance, correlation, and inferences regarding causality. In an associated workshop session the students worked out examples, aided by hand calculators. Some of the special studies undertaken by fourth year students involved the use of assessment techniques and the interpretation of results.

Work on children's development and the ways in which they learn served as a background against which to assess children's progress. At its best, the study of these topics included special tasks in which the students were engaged during their periodic visits to schools, with subsequent follow-up in seminars. For example, students on one course replicated Piagetian investigations designed to explore children's methods of problem solving. In another example, students who had been studying aspects of social development in a class of five year olds compared notes with students who had been observing equivalent characteristics in a class of seven year olds. Written assignments often helped to link theory and practice, and some good examples were based on work with children. In one case, a PGCE student working in a primary school devised simple experiments to explore individual children's number strategies.

The assessment of children's language activities was introduced in all institutions, though there were wide variations in the time and emphasis given to the various elements. Many students had the chance to reflect on their school visits and teaching practice and a number had opportunities to compare samples of children's writing or to study transcripts, video and sound tapes. Most language curriculum courses strongly emphasised the teaching of reading and the use of reading tests, often at the expense of other aspects of language use. While this was a useful introduction to practices which the students will meet in schools, more institutions needed to move beyond this fairly standard diet of reading test investigation to look more closely at a variety of processes which depend upon well-informed observation by the teacher, relating reading, writing, and talk to appropriate teaching strategies. In one institution, the differentiation of work for pupils varying in age, ability and cultural background was a commendable feature of the courses, and the students' written work included practical assignments, frequently involving analysis and evaluation of examples of children's spoken and written language. In another, the students' assessment of children's writing which had been collected during school experience was sharpened by the study of Assessment of Performance Unit (APU) publications on language.[1]

Apart from language, more attention was paid to the assessment of mathematics than of any other area of the curriculum. In one institution students on the mathematics curriculum course were given pages of arithmetic done by children in a local school. They were asked to identify children's weaknesses and to suggest ways to remedy them. In another, students made an evaluation of pupils' understanding of a specific mathematical topic, designing and administering tests to a small group of pupils and subsequently producing a report. Students in a third institution not only examined pupils' written work but also considered the assessment of oral work through tape-recorded interviews. Several courses gave students the opportunity to test individual children's understanding of fundamental ideas such as the conservation of volume when liquid is poured from one container to another. There was rather less evidence of attention to record keeping. Where students were given guided practical experience of assessing pupils' understanding and progress in mathematics they were better able to choose suitable content and teaching methods. However, in about half the mathematics curriculum courses discussion of assessment and the diagnosis of learning difficulties were confined to one or two lectures at most. When these topics were not covered adequately by the course, students often failed to note and identify the cause of pupils' difficulties and were often unclear about what their expectations of pupils should be.

---

[1] For details of these publications write to the APU at the address on page 5

Assessment often featured in science courses, and several institutions creditably introduced students to the work of the Assessment of Performance Unit, which demonstrated approaches to assessment and provided valuable information about children's levels of achievement and teachers' objectives. Some of the work was aimed at helping the students to assess children's acquisition of process skills. For example, in one BEd course the students studied a video recording of children engaged in science activities and were asked to pick out examples of certain skills, such as observation, and to comment on the level of attainment. In another institution, first year BEd students taking a science curriculum course studied the development of children's ability to sort and to classify objects. They then worked with small groups of children of various ages in school, asking them to classify leaves. The results were discussed with their tutor, and the students tried to analyse the strategies and criteria used by the children at different stages of development.

There was little evidence of work on assessment in other areas of the curriculum. A typical example was a physical education curriculum course where the assessment of children's work had very little place. The development of an understanding that successful teaching has to be based on observation of the children and their capacities for movement was scarcely begun. Although a good deal of practical work involved the students in looking at one another's movements, the observations tended to be mechanical and superficial rather than based on a sound understanding of movement. The students' difficulties were compounded by the very limited opportunities to work with children.

As might be expected, the assessment of children's attainments rarely featured in subject studies, though interesting examples were encountered where subject studies and methodology were to be found within the same course. One such, a BEd geography course, involved school visits during which the students carried out assignments such as studying the children's development of spatial awareness, their ability to comprehend maps, the analysis of simple teaching situations, and the use of language which had a specific meaning when used in teaching environmental and geographical topics.

All students were at least introduced to various methods of assessing children's attainment and progress, though coverage was often brief and the diagnostic value of the analysis of children's performance and errors was seldom emphasised sufficiently. Greater attention could be given to helping students to develop diagnostic approaches to their teaching and to practising these in schools rather than simply learning to administer standardised tests. In this respect, it is important that training in assessment techniques should be linked with work on areas of the curriculum which illustrates the range in children's performance, and the progression which might be expected among children in ordinary classes.

No examples were seen of students being introduced to ways in which teachers can review the curriculum they are providing through the use of instruments devised by LEAs.

Meeting the individual needs of pupils

Primary schools are generally organised in mixed ability classes, and the range of ability in an ordinary class is often wide. Many classes include children from more than one age group, as occurs in schools where vertical grouping is practised as a matter of policy, in small schools, or where it is forced upon a school by falling rolls or wide varieties in the size of cohorts. In these classes the range of ability and experience among the children is further extended. This presents a formidable challenge for the training of teachers who have to take account of the individual children's stages of development, ability, and experience when planning, organising, and presenting the work. All the institutions covered some aspects of individual differences, most often those associated with social class, broad developmental stages, children with special needs, and children from ethnic minority groups. Individual differences which were explored less often were differences in motivation, social adjustment, learning styles and giftedness. Much of the work on individual differences occurred as part of education studies. The students' attention was directed to children's characteristics and to organisational features of provision for individual differences such as group work and individual assignments.

The work in curriculum studies was often related to children at particular stages in the primary school, such as younger infants or lower juniors, but there was a tendency for tutors to offer rather general advice about ways of adapting the content and teaching methods to cater for children of different ages and abilities in the same class. In many curriculum courses students were not taught specific strategies and techniques required to provide for the full range of ability and experience they would meet in schools. Sessions of particular value were those where the students studied children's progressive acquisition of particular concepts and skills such as an understanding of time, or reading skills. They gave a sense of direction, helping students to decide on the next steps forward for individual children.

Once students began to observe and to teach primary children they quickly appreciated the practical difficulties that the wide ability range presented. However, an awareness of the challenge did not, of itself, provide solutions. Many institutions used serial school experience to help students to get to grips with the problem. Such work appeared to be most effective when individual students worked with small groups of children with the specific objective of studying individual differences and catering for them. For example, BEd students from one institution each worked with four or five children for a series of weekly sessions and learned a good deal about individual differences, rates of progress, and the levels of work which the children could achieve. In another, one student on the PGCE course taught mathematics to a small group of 5 to 6 year olds as part of a serial school experience. As she gained experience, the class teacher helped her to plan work specifically for the more able and the less able children. Later the student was helped to plan and to teach work on sets to a group of the most able children in the class, to an average group, and to a group of the less able. As the student taught each group, in turn, she made adjustments in the way she presented the tasks and responded to the children.

The training of primary teachers: professional and classroom skills

Occasionally students had an opportunity to study the capabilities of able children and to consider ways of providing for their needs. For example, students worked with individual children in a college mathematics centre an hour a week for three weeks. The children were all of above average ability and some were described as gifted. The students asked to study the children's performance and to explore ways of extending their mathematical skills and understanding.

The work done by students on block teaching practices gave an indication of the extent to which they were able to cater for the range in age, ability and experience within the class. In general, the topics chosen and the material presented were appropriate for the class as a whole. They took account of the children's interests and experience, and the work was often pitched at a reasonable level for the majority of the children. The students were usually able to discuss individual differences within the class in a knowledgeable and perceptive way, but their actual provision of learning experiences did not always reflect their appreciation of these distinctions. In common with many experienced teachers, they found it difficult to cater for the full range of age, ability and experience within the class. The following examples indicate ways in which students were attempting to cater for this range. In one class the children were examining frog spawn which they had collected. The less able were asked to describe what they saw; the more able were required to refine their descriptions and to use scientific terms accurately. For the written record at the end of the lesson two different worksheets had been prepared to make suitable demands on the less able readers and writers as well as on the remainder. This was a modest piece of work, but in planning and in execution it indicated a recognition that work must be adjusted to the different levels of ability.

A PGCE student who had chosen 'materials' as a topic for a class of 8 to 9 year olds employed group work as a way of organising activities to suit children of different abilities. Twelve children, in pairs, were given large sheets of paper and photocopies of illustrations from a book, each showing different stages in the development of a city. They were simply asked to copy the pictures. A group of five children was given a series of pictures of housing from prehistoric times to the present day to copy, while others consulted a reference book on housing, or photocopies of pages from it, to answer questions on a worksheet which the student had prepared. The student managed the groups very well and gave prompt attention to children who required help or who became inattentive. She quickly observed that the book used by one group was difficult for them to read and she concentrated her attention on these children. This was a commendable approach to differentiating the work to match the children's capabilities, but the level and purpose of some of the activities were poorly judged. For example, the children copying pictures found the task undemanding, could see little purpose in it, and soon showed signs of boredom. On the other hand, the worksheets were well designed and neatly presented.

A BEd student on her final teaching practice was seen teaching a lively, often ebullient, class of 34 eleven year olds. The class had been divided into six science groups. Each group was provided with well presented and illustrated work cards, all prepared by the student and carefully tailored to the abilities and interests of the group. A great range of apparatus and materials had been provided, from periscopes, cameras and binoculars to improvised constructions for measuring refraction and reflecting light. Each group also had its own working area, with clues for proceeding carefully posted. Pupils were deeply involved in their experiments and the whole class was urged to record findings under six headings written on the blackboard. Responses to these headings varied considerably but sentences rather than single words were encouraged and the teacher intervened sensitively to help certain groups. The freedom allowed by the student to the groups and their investigations was sometimes abused by a few pupils but she dealt fairly and firmly with recalcitrants. The majority clearly enjoyed the experience and thought 'science with the student was different'. Throughout the lesson the student was relaxed but watchful, moving confidently and purposefully from group to group, quietly redeeming lost causes and rekindling flagging interest with a new point of view.

A third year BEd student gave an excellent explanation of the water cycle, supported by good blackboard work. The class of 8 to 9 year olds was then given cyclostyled sheets, one bearing six numbered diagrams representing stages in the water cycle, the other carrying six statements about the stages. The children had to select the correct statement to fit each diagram and to write it underneath. The student gave concentrated assistance to one of the children who had reading difficulties, and in mathematics she used group work with graded examples drawn from text books. It was clear that the student recognised the need to differentiate the work to cater for the full ability range.

Students were generally aware of the range in ability and experience which they were likely to encounter in primary school classrooms. When attempting to cater for the full range, they met with varying degrees of success. While the mastery of all the necessary skills and techniques depends partly on experience, more could be done to give students in initial training a better foundation. In particular, there is a need to ensure that appropriate skills and techniques are given sufficient emphasis in all curriculum courses and that these are applied during school experience with support and guidance from tutors and class teachers.

Special educational needs

There was considerable variation between institutions in the allocation of time and in the emphasis given to work on special educational needs. The majority had been influenced in their BEd and PGCE course planning by the Warnock Report[1] and the *Education Act 1981* and at the time of the survey many were restructuring their courses in order to take account of the wider definition of special needs given in these documents. The emphasis in these courses tended to be on the teaching of children with special educational needs in the ordinary school but with occasional references to specific disabilities. A small number of other institutions focused solely on slow learners or concentrated on physical or mental disabilities as the main

---

[1] *Special educational needs* HMSO, 1978

components in studies on special educational needs. In three institutions a special BEd (Mencap) was aimed at producing specialists in teaching mentally handicapped children, who could also teach in ordinary schools.

The amount of time devoted to the study of special educational needs and the place of this topic in education studies also varied widely. A small group of institutions relied on the permeation of this work across educational studies in the early part of the courses, followed by options at the end of the second year which continued into the third year. This pattern appeared to result in fragmentation and some students had little or no contact with the topic. Other institutions laid a foundation in the first two years of the BEd degree and built on it by promoting compulsory units, components, or strands devoted to special educational needs in the third and fourth years.

The best examples of coverage of the topic occurred in those numerous institutions which featured it to some extent over the whole four years of the BEd course as an essential element in a number of education studies components, such as child development, educational psychology, and teaching studies. An introduction during the first two years was extended and supported by elements later in the course which offered a sound theoretical framework sustained by school-based work. In one institution, work on special needs was compulsory, with an introductory element embedded in the first year studies of child development. The second year component focused on the implications of the 1981 Act and helped the students to explore the question as to why some children with special needs are educated in special schools rather than in normal schools. Special schools were visited and issues of integration and segregation were discussed. The aim of the third year element was to help the students to develop some of the skills needed to work constructively with children with special needs in ordinary schools. It involved introducing the students to a developmental rating scale and encouraging them to use it while on teaching practice. Part way through the teaching practice, problems experienced by students in their attempts to meet children's special needs were discussed. In about a quarter of the institutions, notably those where the work was not directly applied in schools, treatment of the topic did not appear to be helpful.

The amount and type of work on special educational needs which was covered in curriculum courses varied considerably. Mathematics and language/reading development courses tended to give most attention to this topic, but there was also some in other curriculum areas such as history and science. The most common reference to special needs concerned slow learners and disruptive behaviour. It was rare to find discussion of the wider range of needs which have to be met. An interesting example of the permeation of special needs awareness in curriculum courses was observed when students, following a school visit, presented papers which they had prepared on aspects of classroom organisation, the use of materials, and the planning of activities for children with special needs. The students identified and discussed ways in which these children were influenced by school and class organisation, and they also planned work for the next school visit. Many of the reading courses focused on the particular needs of children diagnosed as poor readers. In one institution, for example, BEd students who were specialising in the education of young children took part in a discussion session which followed their final teaching practice. The discussion was wide ranging, spanning systems of organisation, grouping, remedial support, the withdrawal of children for special teaching, reading difficulties and behaviour problems. The exchange of experiences included references to slow learners, dyslexia, links with parents, and ways of meeting special needs within the integrated day. Disruptive behaviour was a dominant theme.

Many institutions operated on the principle of permeation, and curriculum course tutors referred to special educational needs incidentally rather than treated them as a separate topic. There were only a few examples of work on special needs in curriculum courses dealing with subjects other than mathematics and language; these included an element specifically on teaching the subject or area of the curriculum to children with special educational needs. In one such the aims and objectives of history teaching for children with special needs in infant and primary schools were examined. Where these elements occurred they were often well taught and it may be significant, although the evidence base is small, that where there was good practice there was also a considerable input made by practising teachers from primary schools. In a number of institutions insufficient attention was paid to cross-curricular implications of special educational needs. Definitions of need, curriculum design and delivery were not covered in any depth, and this tended to restrict the ability of students to adapt teaching methods and materials across the curriculum.

There were only a few examples of references being made to special educational needs in specialist subject courses. In a geography lecture to second year BEd students, for example, the place of visual images in the teaching of geography was considered and, in particular, the use of graphicacy as an alternative route to learning which can help those with learning difficulties. The wider definition of special educational needs pervaded the whole of the session. Students were most easily helped to appreciate ways of adapting work in their specialist subjects where their knowledge and confidence were greatest.

If a permeative approach across the curriculum is to be effective there would appear to be a need for explicit arrangements for coordinating special educational needs in curriculum course planning and for specific objectives to be laid down to guide this approach. The lack of these arrangements in some institutions led to repetition and overlap of content and occasionally to confusion about the definition of special needs. For example, students in one institution were introduced to a consideration of special educational needs in two ways. First, it appeared to permeate a variety of topics about schools, children, and the curriculum; second, it was introduced directly through specific elements in their course. Senior staff saw special educational needs as a priority area and the amount of attention given to it overall was greater than that found in many institutions. Much of the work was noteworthy: the construction of various modules, the various teaching approaches used by tutors and the quality of their teaching, the close links between taught elements and school experience, and the quality of students' assignments. Yet, in both the specific and the permeative elements, some confusion was evident amongst tutors on precisely what definition of special educational needs was to be employed. In some of the specific elements it was seen as largely concerning disabled children and, as often as not, the more severely disabled. In others the definition was much wider and included socially disadvantaged children. The same confusion of definition was found in the permeative elements. There was also some uncertainty noted on whether all children with special educational needs were now to be integrated into ordinary schools and classes or whether some would still be catered for in separate units and schools. Students' uncertainties reflected these confusions. Some had grasped the implications of the wider definition while others still saw special educational needs primarily in terms of severe disability. Among the students there was a widespread misunderstanding of the national recommendations about integration, and an understandable fear about the consequences of total integration. In addition to a need for greater coordination, there appears to be a need for a sharper focus to the work, particularly in curriculum courses, if students are to acquire the skills necessary to provide for children with special educational needs in ordinary classes. These institutions had a core of interested and informed staff, though the extent to which the tutors who taught education studies, curriculum courses and subject studies were equipped to teach in the area of special educational needs varied considerably.

At the time of the survey a few institutions still perceived special educational needs largely in terms of mental or physical disabilities, or offered courses which were directed mainly towards educating slow learners. For example, in one institution work in special educational needs occurred chiefly in the third year of the BEd, when students were offered an option on slow learners. Observation of course work, lectures, and the students' work in schools indicated that the content was very narrowly conceived. It was predominantly based on remedial teaching materials and techniques of limited value and applicability, to the neglect of wider and more important issues which would have been appropriate for students in initial training. Such courses were designed upon an earlier and narrower definition of special educational needs than that which is currently employed, and they are in need of revision.

The structure of the BEd (Mencap) courses tended to be bipartite with half of the course devoted to work with children who have one specific disability in a special school and half to training for general class teaching in ordinary schools. The specialised focus of these courses resulted in students receiving limited experience of teaching in ordinary schools and restricted coverage of the primary school curriculum. Their structure did not lend itself to producing teachers able to function equally well in special schools and in ordinary schools, but some good practice was observed in the teaching of the courses.

Ethnic diversity

All the institutions recognised the need to give students an understanding of the implications for primary schools of the ethnic diversity in British society. A substantial number were reviewing their policies and revising their course content and structures with this in mind. Most of the work formed part of education studies, whether taught as part of the general course or as distinct units. Approximately one third of the institutions gave considerable time and emphasis to multi-ethnic issues, though there was marked variation in the amount of time allocated to a compulsory core and to options. Some institutions provided short compulsory courses ranging from 8 to 30 hours: many offered further, optional courses to build on these. A minority paid insufficient attention to education for a multi-ethnic society. A very small number of institutions offered an optional course in teaching English as a second language.

The options in education for a multi-ethnic society were frequently substantial; for example, one institution provided an optional course of 180 hours which built on a core course of 30 hours. In about half the institutions these options were set against other important aspects, such as special needs, education in the early years, or curriculum subjects. There were indications that when this occurred the students frequently felt that the subject options would be of more benefit to them professionally. In one case half the year group chose the multi-ethnic option in one year, but the course did not run in the following year because too few students selected it. In some institutions the BEd multi-ethnic option was available only to honours students. Some institutions which offered only a slender compulsory component claimed that this was compensated for by a policy of permeation whereby multi-ethnic aspects were covered as appropriate in many parts of the BEd and the PGCE courses. Although in about half the institutions multi-ethnic education was given some measure of attention, either in main subject studies or in professional studies, there was little evidence to support this assertion. These various arrangements resulted in some students covering a good deal of ground in multi-ethnic issues and others very little.

Some of the best work occurred where students studied multi-ethnic aspects through a combination of compulsory component, an option, and carefully planned attention to them, as appropriate, in other parts of the BEd and PGCE courses, such as curriculum studies and subject studies.

There tended to be more explicit consideration of multi-ethnic issues in institutions which were situated in inner-city areas where the ethnic diversity of the population heightened the students' awareness. In some of these, where interest in multi-ethnic issues was a strong feature of the work, the tutors aimed to ensure that the students were knowledgeable about them and also that they could recognise and provide for the needs of children from ethnic minorites. They often claimed that students needed to be aware of certain issues before the first block teaching practice, and studies therefore had to begin early in the course. Provision was most successful where lectures and seminars were supported by serial school experience and when good use was made of local resources. A good example noted was that of a conference which used video material beamed to small discussion groups consisting of a tutor, visiting teachers, students and social workers. A particularly lively discussion was led by five teachers who drew upon the students' school experience. Language difficulties were considered and valuable help was given by a Hindi teacher. The institution's courses commendably reflected discussion in consultative committees which consisted of tutors, teachers, social workers, leaders of ethnic groups, and community figures in race relations: all had worked towards designing courses which would help to promote mutual understanding and provide experience firmly related to the professional development of teachers. In several institutions, college-based work was well supported with both practical and written assignments as well as experience with children who had special language needs. The student bodies of some institutions reflected a rich multi-lingual background which could, on occasions, have a practical influence on the work of some of the students as primary school teachers, for example in the assessment of reading material for second language learners. Students training in areas of culturally diverse population had opportunities to work with ethnic minority pupils on both serial visits and block teaching practices. The multi-ethnic emphasis in the course content and structure in many institutions in these areas was well received by students and was a considerable advantage to them in their work in schools.

Students leaving training institutions may work as teachers in any part of the country. Institutions increasingly recognised the need to prepare students to educate all children for life in an ethnically diverse society and also to introduce them to the particular needs of children from ethnic minority groups. Those situated in parts of the country where the population contained very few families from ethnic minorities found it difficult to give students opportunities to learn at first hand about the needs and characteristics of different ethnic groups and to ensure that students had some experience in multi-ethnic primary schools. Although one or two institutions made considerable efforts to enable students to visit multi-ethnic areas, such good intentions were often constrained by a shortage of both time and finance. Much of the work in such institutions therefore tended to be rather theoretical, with little or no opportunity for school-based work in appropriate circumstances. However, care was generally taken where possible to relate theory to classroom practice. For example, third year students in an institution situated in a rural area considered ways of preparing children in schools without ethnic minority groups for life in an ethnically diverse society. They considered the use of project work to study and compare different cultures, learning through correspondence with minority group children in schools in other areas, and through visiting speakers. Aspects of dance and drama were discussed as well as the need to recognise and provide for individual differences. Such work could have been better supported, possibly by the provision of resource centres similar to those found in ethnically diverse areas which provided good coverage of African and Asian cultures. A few institutions in areas which lacked ethnic minority groups made good use of urban study centres where students were able to gain experience of multi-ethnic communities during residential weeks, and these provided a valuable focus for other course work. While there were some examples of good practice, there was considerable variation in the content and methodology of courses on education in a mulit-ethnic society. It was unfortunate to find in some institutions an approach which associated the teaching of pupils from ethnic minority groups with the courses on children with learning difficulties and those who were under-achieving.

Quality in schools: the initial training of teachers

In addition to courses devoted specifically to multi-ethnic issues the topic was given some consideration in the majority of religious studies courses, in both the main subject and the professional components. One course was described by students as dynamic and making great demands on them. It included a discussion of school assemblies, focusing upon the idea that these have an integrative function, and a number of students prepared assemblies in schools which reflected the work they had done in college. Students in another institution were introduced to differences in culture and background in several communities; not only did they study these in college, but also through a wide range of visits and fieldwork which had given them first hand experience in two cities.

Valuable aspects of the ethnic studies were frequently encountered within main course history, geography and humanities. For example, they arose in one institution as part of geography fieldwork in multi-ethnic areas of England and in Tunisia. In another institution the environmental studies component included a helpful if small input on the history of immigrant communities in London, and the contribution they had made. Another excellent example was observed in a humanities session on cultural contrasts, where students studied southern Indian performance art and learned some dances. This practical work, which was well supported with a tape/slide sequence, combined rigorous learning about another culture and material which could be applied in school.

Isolated examples of multi-ethnic topics occurred in other professional courses; for example, music typically included styles of music from other cultures and a physical education group discussed ways in which multi-ethnic considerations affected the teaching of physical education in the primary school. Multi-ethnic variety featured most prominently in the professional components of language courses, where some institutions gave it considerable attention. One session on story telling began with the tutor leading a discussion which illustrated the use of Punjabi before reading a story which provided an excellent model for students. He offered good advice on story telling in general and also explored some of the factors to be considered in the choice of stories for children. In another institution the topic of language in the multi-ethnic classroom included a discussion of the teaching of bilingual children and mother tongue teaching, with students contributing from their own personal experience. The content was well supported with a consideration of the resources and range of teaching approaches needed to provide for children's individual needs.

The work was influenced by the experience of the staff. In the majority of institutions there was considerable dependence upon outside speakers. For example, in one valuable session an Asian youth and a community worker described various aspects of the latter's work: teaching O-level Bengali in a comprehensive school, taking Asian teenagers on a visit to Bangladesh, teaching Bengali to teachers, and visiting the local school in her role as a social worker. As a means of obtaining insight into some aspects of Asian culture and problems experienced by Asians in this country, this session was highly successful. In some cases, too heavy a reliance on visiting speakers meant that a systematic development of understanding was very difficult to achieve.

Nursery education

Primary courses often cover a wide age range, from children of three in nursery provision to the 11 to 12 year olds who are soon to transfer to secondary schools. This wide age span inevitably creates problems for institutions in course planning. While some features of learning and teaching are common to the whole primary age range, many aspects of curriculum content, organisation, and teaching approaches are sufficiently different to require explicit consideration in relation to the differing needs of nursery, younger primary, and older primary children.

A quarter of the institutions offered a primary course which included a nursery component covering the 3 to 5 age range. Only a minority of these courses provided adequate training for nursery teachers. In those institutions which focused on the 3 to 8 age range, the emphasis with few exceptions was on the 5 to 8 year olds. A common pattern was to provide an option on 'nursery education' or 'nursery-infant curriculum' in the third or fourth year, with too little attention being paid to the specific needs of nursery children in the first two years of the course. The emphasis placed on the 5 to 8 age range often discouraged students from choosing an option on the pre-school years, particularly when it was set against curriculum courses which the students felt could help them to develop a curricular strength. By contrast, in one institution where nursery provision was good, the nursery-infant group focused on the 3 to 7 age range for all their professional work and this was supported by a substantial nursery option in the third year. These students also had the opportunity to spend one or two periods of teaching practice in nursery schools and nursery classes in other schools.

Approximately half the institutions were able to provide students with school experience that included such placements. A few institutions lacked nursery provision in their locality and this made it necessary for students to live away during block practice or face long journeys to gain experience with the under fives. The students in several institutions benefited from the presence of a nursery school or a playgroup on site. In one example, first year BEd students visited the college playgroup regularly and the visits were profitably linked to the curriculum courses in language and mathematics. In another, practical work in an excellent nursery school provided shared experience on which to base subsequent group discussions about the nursery curriculum. In one or two institutions the accommodation was designed to enable students to work with very young children. For example, a spacious room was used as a nursery-infant centre and equipped with suitable furniture and resources. It allowed the students and staff to explore different ways of organising resources and of presenting and displaying children's work. Various dispositions of furniture and equipment were tried with groups of young children and teaching approaches were practised. The room was also used for lectures and seminars.

In the majority of curriculum courses for the 3 to 8 age range, much of the content and methodology was more appropriate for older infants. For example, not enough emphasis was placed on the use of natural materials such as sand, water, clay and wood, and the essential topic of play and its role in the education of young children was frequently given only superficial treatment. Quite often this bias could be linked to the tutors' own teaching experience, since few had worked with the under-fives. This lack of experience was also evident during teaching practice when students in nursery classes were frequently supervised by tutors with an inadequate knowledge of the age group. Sometimes greater use could have been made of existing knowledge and skills. In one case 16 students were placed in nursery schools and classes for their final teaching practice, but only two of them were supervised by the one experienced nursery tutor.

Some of the best work in curriculum courses occurred when they were closely linked to school experience, enabling the students to relate theory to practice. For example, in one session students discussed practical activities in mathematics for very young children who were not yet able to read and write. The students sorted and sequenced materials, using a good range of apparatus; they considered questions which might be put to children to guide their learning and probe their understanding; and they discussed some of the words which would be used. All of this was related to the problems of matching the work to the capabilities of individual children. Nursery options provided examples of well-chosen topics such as the educational potential of basic play materials. For example, two third year students led a discussion on the use of clay and wood. Their talk was illustrated with examples from teaching practice and useful advice was given regarding the presentation, handling, and educational use of these materials.

All the nursery courses gave some attention to the role of nursery nurses and ancillary staff, liaison with support services, relationships with parents, and building up the students' knowledge of young children's development. These elements appeared mainly in the optional courses in the third and fourth years. The majority of the institutions needed to give more time and better coordinated attention to these matters throughout the course.

Many of the observations made about the training of teachers for work with nursery children also applied to courses which prepared students to teach the 4 to 7 age range. The increasing number of four year olds in primary classes makes it essential that institutions give serious attention to this age group. These very young children require a programme similar to that for nursery children, but only a few institutions equipped primary students to meet their needs.

Relationships with parents and the wider community

The role of parents was considered in the majority of courses, especially in those relating to nursery education and to the early years. Students came into contact with parents where there was a nursery class or play group on the campus, and on teaching practice. The emphasis in training was usually on parents' relationships with their children, their role in supporting the children's education and development, and their use as helpers in schools. References to parents, and to relationships between schools and the community, were generally made in work on child development, in education studies concerned with the sociological aspects of home, school and community, in courses on special educational needs, and in components dealing with multi-ethnic issues.

There was some good work taking place. For example, some students observed families with young children in playgrounds and in other public places and noted their activities and parent-child interaction. The data was used in a seminar on the knowledge, skills, and experiences which children acquire out of school and the influence of parents on these. There were four or five examples of role play being used to help students to understand parents' views and to learn to negotiate with them. In a BEd language curriculum course students acted out, in groups, a teacher discussing a child's written work with his parents. The observers noted the strategies used and the perceptions conveyed by the actors, and these were analysed and discussed. Students in one college benefited from a research project which was located in the college. This involved parents in the education of pre-school children and the students worked alongside the parents in school. In one institution particularly good use was made of the mature students' experience as parents while another emphasised the value of the course to students as future parents.

School experience offered a potentially rich source of contacts with parents. For example, at the beginning of their third year, BEd students following a curriculum course in environmental studies spent a fortnight in a rural school where they taught small groups of children. The work was centred on a local study. At the end of the period the students set up a display of the children's work and invited the parents to see it. The students talked informally with parents about the purpose of the work and about the children's progress. This gave the students experience of explaining to parents what had been done, as well as an opportunity to appreciate the parents' views and interests. However, in general, few students on teaching practice were asked to comment on contacts with parents. Their teaching practice notebooks frequently indicated an awareness of the children's background and the social context of the school, but institutions rarely required more than very general statements.

A minority made more explicit demands; for example, a group of first year BEd students on weekly serial visits were required to note in some detail the school's relationship with the community and with the parents, and this was followed up later with work on links between home and school. On teaching practice it appeared to be left mostly to individual students and schools to initiate contacts between students and parents. While some schools encouraged contacts, one group of students reported that they had been 'sheltered' from parents by their teaching practice schools. Students teaching the youngest children tended to have more frequent contacts with parents than those teaching older children, particularly if the school had an 'open door' policy which encouraged parents to accompany their children into the classroom. In a few cases students took part in extra-curricular school activities, educational visits, and social and fund raising events which also involved parents and the community. Students generally welcomed such opportunities to meet parents. In sum, most institutions gave some attention to home-school relationships, but the extent of coverage varied widely and it was exceptional to find students acquiring a detailed understanding of the topic. When it did occur it was most likely to be found in early years courses.

Institutions varied in the extent to which they prepared students for the variety of community contexts in which they might begin their professional careers. Work in education studies usually examined the implications of social and environmental issues such as social disadvantage, the expectations and attitudes of upwardly mobile social groups, and the influence on families of inner city conditions.

A few institutions, by virtue of their location, were able to give the students practical experience in schools stituated in contrasting social and environmental contexts. However, many institutions had access to only a limited range. Some of these institutions made special arrangements for the students to gain first hand experience of work in areas which contrasted with those normally met on their routine school experience. For example, a small number situated in rural areas arranged for a proportion of their students to visit urban study centres, some for observation but others for a period of teaching practice and community work. A minority of other institutions arranged shorter visits to the nearest urban centres where the students gained some experience of work in the inner city. One or two colleges invited groups of children from inner city areas for short residential periods. In one institution, attempts were made to draw the students' attention to features of the children's linguistic performance, through visits to schools and by bringing in children from other areas. There was some good work in a fourth year BEd group, where the students were asked to compare their experience in a country school near to the college with their experience in an inner city school in London. No examples were encountered of institutions in large urban conurbations sending students into rural areas to acquaint themselves with features of the work in one- and two-teacher schools and with the experiences of children who grow up in rural isolation. In giving students some experience with children who live in areas unfamiliar to them, the institutions tended to emphasise social and behavioural issues rather than curricular implications for the schools serving such areas.

In several institutions students were encouraged to participate in the activities of the local community and this was made easier where the institutions themselves acted as cultural centres and the students were able to meet informally with adults who were not professionally engaged in education.

Classroom relationships and control

Classroom relationships and control generally formed part of the work in education and professional studies but they were also covered in various ways in some curriculum courses and in school experience, at the preparation stage, in the schools, or in follow-up discussions.

The work in education studies varied not only from one institution to another but also from one tutor to another within the same institution. The following examples will serve to illustrate the variety. In one PGCE session, the tutor did little more than listen sympathetically to students' expressions of their own anxieties about class control. In a BEd lecture in the same institution, the tutors were attempting to draw on behavioural theory to help some 50 second year students to structure their teaching, but did so by showing an American film that served only to alienate many of the students both from the techniques being applied and the principles underlying them. Much more successful was a follow-up seminar, run by one of the same team of tutors for some of the same students. The students were presented with written case studies depicting classroom problems; they divided into discussion groups to draw on behavioural techniques in devising solutions, and the solutions proposed by different groups were compared at the end of the session.

Some helpful integrative approaches to this topic were seen in a number of other institutions. In one, for example, each member of a third year BEd group had identified a child presenting her with control problems during teaching practice. Making use of a college-designed booklet on devising and evaluating strategies for changing behaviour, each student devised a programme and the tutor saw the students in groups of three to discuss the programmes being developed. These more positive approaches were clearly of value to the students, but the work could have been enhanced by a further extension into practice, with students being observed and advised as they tried out their programmes in the classroom. College tutors recognised the value of such extension but tended to be inhibited by what they saw as its cost implications.

It was often difficult to find how students were taught general control techniques such as the use of the voice and eyes, positioning, changing from one activity to another, and dealing with interruptions. Sometimes these were referred to in education studies, and sometimes they were touched upon in curriculum courses, for example in discussing class control when children are moving freely in a large space during physical education lessons. They also arose in connection with school experience, for example when students raised questions with tutors and teachers about control. Evidence from students observed on teaching practice suggests that practically all the students established good relationships with the children in their classes and few experienced difficulties of control.

Other issues

Almost all the institutions introduced students to the structure of the education system as a whole, paying most attention to provision for children aged 3 to 18 years. Education studies generally examined some of the influences and constraints on the system and its relationship to the community at large. Interesting sessions included group discussion following a visit by a tutor and fourth year BEd students to a Select Committee to observe the Secretary of State for Education and Science giving evidence; a talk given by a chief education officer, followed by discussion of the LEA's curricular guidelines; seminars on major reports on education; a session on determinants of the curriculum; and one on present trends in the state system.

There were only isolated instances of institutions extending the students' understanding of industry and the world of work, and relating this to the education of children in primary schools. One institution, for example, described its aims as to give to students: an awareness and respect for the world of work; recognition of the educational possibilities in technological advances; a sympathy towards the business of producing goods and services; and a sense of responsibility for transmitting their awareness and understanding to the children they teach.

The first year BEd students visited local museums, factories, and industrial archaeological sites. Some had further opportunities for industrial visits arising from subject studies or in connection with curriculum courses. Field work for students of art, drama, geography and history was well established and sometimes it included industrial visits; in one example, groups of students had been to a working mill and to a forge. The students and the children with whom they were working had together spoken to millers, electricians and plumbers while they were about their work. This had been followed up in school and had occasionally led to topic work in science. Links between another college and the Primary Industry Education Project led to liaison with local firms and the generation of support materials which the students found of considerable use. Despite a few such positive examples at least one college believed that a consideration of the world of work was not necessary on primary courses, and many others ignored it.

7 The training of secondary teachers

Context

Initial teacher training courses at secondary level were offered by 19 of the 30 institutions included in the survey. These courses covered both the 11 to 16 and the 11 to 18 age groups, and they reflected, in structure and content, the differing avenues of study which are open to intending secondary teachers.

The Bachelor of Education (BEd) degree at secondary level accounts for only 22 per cent of total secondary provision, all other training for this phase being by the PGCE route. BEd courses are currently limited to a small number of specialist subjects, and the 15 BEd subject courses inspected in the survey involved only seven different subjects. Ten of the 15 subject courses visited were in three of these subjects, which represent the majority of secondary BEd provision; namely home economics, physical education, and craft, design and technology. Other visits were to mathematics, religious education, and science, and to courses in English as a second or subsidiary subject.

As implied above, the range of subjects available to intending secondary teachers is wider in postgraduate courses, and 13 different subjects were inspected in the 16 PGCE courses included in the survey; namely, art, drama, English, geography, history, home economics, mathematics, modern languages, music, physical education, religious education, science and social studies. However, the majority of secondary teachers are trained through PGCE courses provided within the university sector, which lay outside the scope of this survey. There were, therefore, fewer opportunities for any overall assessment of secondary training than for that of primary training, and it should be emphasised that the evidence base for the observations in the sections that follow is correspondingly more limited.

Within these constraints, it was noticeable that overall course structures varied considerably between institutions, both in BEd and PGCE. General aims for the training of teachers were often outlined in prospectuses and course submissions but there was little evidence of detail, and the aims and objectives of secondary courses, particularly relating to the BEd, were sometimes not clearly distinguished from those of primary courses.

Quality in schools: the initial training of teachers

As indicated earlier in the report, there is a definable range of essential issues which face the training institution in its programme of specialist and professional work for the new secondary teacher. The evidence of this survey suggests that there is, in general, wide agreement on these issues in institutions as providing a framework for course programmes at secondary level. With varying degrees of success, the institutions sought to ensure that the students were well equipped and confident in their knowledge of their specialist subject, practised in various methods of teaching it, and able to fulfil the important pastoral role of looking after the overall welfare of the pupils entrusted to their care. To this end they helped students to develop a mastery of teaching skills, which included planning and organising classroom activities and developing an awareness of pupils' individual needs. In the best examples, students were helped to assess the progress of their pupils and keep informative records, adjust their work to match variations in ability, and appraise their own effectiveness. Additionally, the courses often considered such aspects as the relationship between language and learning; ways in which the teaching of a subject can contribute to the personal and social development of pupils; the contribution of the student's main subject to the secondary school curriculum as a whole; and the use of more recent technological developments. The value which students obtained from this work was enhanced in those institutions where they learned about the teaching of their specialisms against a background of a developing understanding of the educational system as a whole and of the place of schools in society, including the relationship of schools with parents and the community generally. Further benefit was obtained from linking these issues across relevant elements within the BEd or PGCE courses and especially from closely relating college activities with practical work in schools. In helping students towards an understanding of their pastoral role, institutions recognised that its foundation must rest on the development of good relations with pupils. Many courses also offered students help in relating their work to the outside world, to the work of other professionals, and to the needs of young adults.

There was a wide variation in the approaches used in the courses to develop the students' ability to meet all these demands, and in the depth and extent of the coverage. The quality and effectiveness of the preparation of secondary specialist teachers are considered in the following sections.

Selection of students

BEd courses

If students are to derive maximum benefit from the course and to make an effective contribution as teachers in secondary schools, the quality of the selection process is critical. With the restrictions on the range of subjects retained for the BEd secondary course, most of those inspected were in areas of the curriculum where there is a shortage of specialist teachers, or were subjects which have a considerable practical element. In the case of the shortage subjects there was a relatively small number of candidates with adequate academic qualifications from which institutions could select. In the case of the practical subjects, consideration had also to be given to skills other than academic performance.

In the majority of cases the criteria and procedure for selecting candidates to study the main subjects were adequate, and in assessing the merits of applicants for practical subjects some institutions exercised considerable ingenuity. The procedures for choosing physical education students in one college were especially thorough. Candidates were called for interviews and tests which were spread over two days. Interviews were conducted by the head of the subject department, or the course coordinator, and teachers from a panel which had been formed following consultation with LEA advisers. Candidates had two individual interviews and took part in a group interview. They were also involved in practical activities including dance, gymnastics, swimming, and a game of their own choice, during which they were watched by tutors and a teacher.

However, the effect of the limited level of academic qualifications of applicants was very evident in some of the shortage subject courses. A number of the students had either very low A-level grades in the subject or only an O-level grade. There were examples of such students in teaching groups alongside others with better qualifications, and the pace of the work was too slow to challenge the more knowledgeable sufficiently. Some students were lacking the necessary background to tackle the demands of the course.

The selection of students for some of the second or subsidiary subject studies gave cause for concern. Students were normally accepted for BEd secondary courses on the strength of their main subject, but not all had the further qualifications necessary to follow a second subject appropriately, especially when the available range was limited. Some college regulations stated that there were no specific admission requirements for the subsidiary course, one of them indicating that 'the students' backgrounds and interests will be explored at interview'. There were students whose initial qualification in their subsidiary subject was inadequate to enable them to obtain full benefit from the course, or to provide an adequate basis for their subsequent teaching of the subject. In one institution many of those taking English as a second subject had achieved only a lower grade at O-level. In another college, only about half of the students taking mathematics as a subsidiary subject had an A-level qualification in the subject.

In general, the treatment of the main subject in range and depth was considered to be well suited to the level of the students' understanding, except in those sessions where the wide range of achievement in a group inhibited the pace of the work for those with better initial qualifications. In one course where students with inadequate starting qualifications had been recruited, the content of the main subject study proved difficult for them to follow and to understand.

PGCE courses
For each secondary PGCE subject offered by an institution there is a precise

105

allocation of target places. The targets for the popular subjects like English and history were easily reached by the survey institutions and in general there was a good match with the degree subjects offered by the candidates. It was found much more difficult to fill the places for the shortage subjects such as mathematics, science, and religious education, and some places remained unfilled. The range of degree subjects accepted for secondary mathematics included: experimental psychology, religious education, sociology and history. In many cases it was difficult to see the justification for such acceptance, since the short PGCE course offers little opportunity to remedy students' deficiencies in subject knowledge. Some students took a subsidiary as well as a main subject, generally in an area related to the main subject or complementary to it. The range of subsidiary subjects was generally wider than the list of main subjects and sometimes included topics such as pastoral care. The normal requirement for admission to a subsidiary subject course was a substantial base in the student's degree or at least a pass in an appropriate A-level. However, in one institution students were following second subject courses without even an A-level background.

In about half the courses the criteria for the selection of candidates were appropriate, and the procedures for selection effectively carried out, but a small number of the cases gave cause for concern. The most common reservation related to the absence of subject tutors at interviews. Some colleges ran general selection interviews without reference to the particular subject and relied on personality and motivation as the main criteria, assuming that if the degree subject was appropriate that of itself would ensure suitability for admission to the method course. A number of science courses appeared to have no specific requirements beyond the institution's general admission criteria, and in one college the history tutor had no hand in the selection of history students. There were a few examples of very late entrants being accepted on the basis of their degree, without interview. In a few instances the interview was not sufficiently rigorous; in the case of a modern languages course, for instance, 10 minutes' conversation in a foreign language provided no more than a token test of fluency. Conversely, in another modern languages course, students were rejected if their competence in a second language was inadequate even where the degree and the fluency in the first language were good. In contrast to these examples, there were many instances of effective selection procedures which indicated that the colleges were selecting their PGCE students efficiently.

There were a number of cases where the selection process was particularly impressive. One example was a drama course, where the staff were anxious that applicants should fully understand the aims and nature of the course. Selection occupied a full day, and groups of applicants were shown a video recording of a drama lesson and received a sample teaching session. There were group and individual discussions of what had taken place during the day, and staff assessed how responsive and sensitive the students were to what they had seen. Another excellent example was a physical education course, where considerable effort was made to ensure that students entered with the most suitable undergraduate experience. Course literature emphasised that the first degree must comprise a major study of PE, not merely an ancillary one, and indicated examples of degrees such as leisure studies which were unlikely to be acceptable. Since insufficient detail was available from the normal application forms, students had to complete a supplementary form giving information on the precise content of their degree, on practical achievements, and on motivation. A full day's selection procedure involved group discussions, meetings with current students, practical sessions in gymnastics and dance, and two interviews with a panel comprising a serving teacher and two college staff. This college clearly was at great pains to make its selection procedure comprehensive and effective. Another case, in mathematics, illustrated profitable cooperation between college staff and teachers. Candidates were interviewed by a tutor together with a head of department from a local secondary school. The two complemented one another well, and sensitively probed each applicants' motivation and interests. They were particularly successful in assessing the candidates' likely capacity to adjust to the rigours and demands of teaching, and their suitability for training. An economics and social studies course placed great emphasis upon group activities during its interviews. Groups of applicants had to address themselves to a particular problem and exercise collective reasoning and judgement in determining an appropriate solution. College staff observed candidates' ability to relate to one another and to apply their knowledge. The results of this useful practical exercise were then used to supplement information gleaned from individual interviews.

In general, the academic quality of PGCE students was high, with three-quarters of the secondary students having a second class honours degree or better. Most institutions recruited their students from a wide area and from among graduates of a wide variety of institutions: universities, polytechnics and colleges. An interesting feature of some PGCE intakes was the extent to which institutions recruited their own graduates, and in one case as many as a quarter of the students were from the institution's own BA/BSc courses.

The degree background of PGCE students

In general, and outside the shortage subjects cited earlier, there was a good match between the degree qualifications of students and the courses for which they were enrolled, and a similar coincidence between degree subjects and likely subsequent teaching duties in the secondary school. In some cases there was an exact match. In one French course all 10 students had a second class honours degree in French; one history course had recruited only history graduates in each of its last two entry groups; and two institutions had only geography graduates on their geography courses. In some other cases there was not such a close match, though the majority of students were still well qualified.

There was a small number of students who had entered PGCE from degree courses which were not the most appropriate for intending specialist secondary teachers. A special case was sometimes made for the orientation of a particular degree, the institution exercising judgement on whether, for instance, a psychology or engineering degree course had a sufficient mathematics weighting. In a sense the individual student in such circumstances can be easily identified and counselled, though it was not clear that this was regularly happening. In a much larger number of cases, students had pursued undergraduate studies which by nomenclature were perfectly acceptable, but whose content inevitably left some gaps in what would be needed for teaching in the secondary school. In history, for example, where considerable differences in content are to be found from one undergraduate course to another, students were often deficient in knowledge of certain periods (such as medieval history) or themes (such as world or local history) which are commonly taught in schools. A comparable situation could be found in any given cohort of English graduates. More suprisingly, it was found in several cases that a French degree was no guarantee of the oral fluency necessary for future school work. Similarly, in a PGCE drama course recruited almost exclusively from drama graduates there was no guarantee that the undergraduate studies of all the students had included any appreciation of the aesthetics of the theatre. In this institution, a case lore had been built up on which degrees were the most suitable basis for specialist postgraduate training. Yet the college did not appear to build this judgment into any remedial or compensatory action to assist those who had been identified as lacking knowledge in particular subjects.

There were other instances of lack of attention to the deficiencies in knowledge and expertise which characterised some incoming graduates, but a small number of courses did respond effectively to this need. Just a few examples of such courses may be cited. In one instance a biology elective was available for science students who were deficient in that field and who wished to be able to teach general science in the lower secondary years. One home economics course ran 'compensatory studies' in the different fields of the discipline where students felt inadequately equipped by their previous studies. One mathematics course contained work on matrices, specifically for the benefit of those with limited expertise. In a different vein, one history course sensitively chose its examples in methodological work from subject areas which many students had not come across before. This was a useful way of introducing students to new and relevant material which would undoubtedly benefit them later and was a strategy that could beneficially have been replicated elsewhere. It would be unrealistic to expect institutions in the time available to be able to compensate fully for gaps in students' knowledge. To an extent all teachers have to prepare themselves individually for a large part of the school syllabus, and students must expect to make the necessary extension of their academic competence. Nevertheless, institutions could do far more than at present to alert students to their likely subject needs and to guide them in making up any potential deficiencies.

Development of teaching skills

The subject specialist role

All the institutions recognised the importance of the subject method component as that part of the course where students developed the ability to teach their specialist subject. The best of the courses aimed not only to develop in the students the specific skills and understanding that this role demands, but to set these within a context of wider professional issues. The following sections consider various aspects of this process and the extent to which institutions were effectively addressing them.

Classroom methods and approaches

In about three-quarters of the PGCE subject method courses and in about two-thirds of those in BEd, students were judged to be gaining a good grasp of the approaches and methods appropriate to the successful teaching of the subject. In a substantial number of these (one-third of PGCE and half of BEd courses) the preparation of students for their role was considered to be particularly commendable. However, it is of some concern that in a minority of cases the provisions for specialist preparation had serious deficiencies.

There were some very good examples of subject method courses which were soundly designed and taught, and which were using practical experience within schools to particularly good advantage. One such was a PGCE mathematics course where the staff provided a good grounding in how pupils learn the subject. Discussion of concept development was supported by illustrations from particular mathematics topics, and tutors encouraged students to present pupils with stimulating material and to use microcomputers in their teaching. In another PGCE mathematics course, students were provided with a variety of activities which included a discussion of the teaching of a particular mathematics lesson and its objectives, other types of mathematics lessons which might be practised, and the resources available for teaching the subject. The work included planning and simulated delivery of exemplar lessons, and students were provided with opportunities to consider the strategies for teaching a given topic, analysing and sequencing the concepts and techniques. Other aspects of the topic studies were record-keeping, the importance of exploratory talk by pupils, and the use of audio-visual and published material.

In another PGCE course, modern languages students were provided with an understanding of the methodology of their subjects through school visits with related assignments, the use of teaching materials prepared by the tutor as working examples (issued to each student for the duration of the course), an evaluation of school language courses, and peer group teaching. A head of department from a local school spoke about the resources and methodology of sixth form modern languages teaching, and the programme as a whole provided an excellent treatment of the subject, thoroughly practical, pitched exactly at the appropriate level, and of considerable help to new teachers.

There were some equally good examples of how students learn to teach their specialist subjects in the BEd course. Specialist home economics tutors in one institution helped students develop an understanding of teaching the subject through various activities which included the use of micro-teaching in the students' groups and contact with pupils brought into the institution from local schools. In a carefully organised and structured mathematics method course for BEd students, there was constant concern for their mathematical education, well aligned with a continuous emphasis on the application of the subject in the classroom. Students in both main and subsidiary method groups were involved in the presentation of lessons and in the leading of seminars. From these opportunities and from the examples of the methods used by tutors, the students gained a good foundation for teaching the subject.

Another example was a PE course for BEd students, where the whole of the first year group of 40 students, with the support of five tutors, was involved with about 70 children from local primary schools in working through a variety of practical activities. The children were taught by groups of students who had carefully prepared the work, while other students critically watched and completed observation schedules. This commendable enterprise had been carefully prepared by tutors, teachers and students, and the observations were constructively used in follow-up discussions.

There were a few examples where students were obtaining a much more limited opportunity for teaching their subjects. The limitations of students on one such course, PGCE for RE specialists, were revealed in their inability on teaching practice to define clearly their objectives, and in their failure to develop techniques for organising class discussion or to evaluate resources appropriately. There was some lack of rigour in the course and this no doubt contributed to these difficulties. In one PGCE drama method course, the hesitancy and uncertainty of the tutor's presentation led to a lack of student confidence, and there was inadequate attention to the available range of teaching approaches. Similar limitations were noted in a PGCE modern language course. Students made few visits to schools, and even these were made without an accompanying tutor. This inhibited any sensible follow-up discussion, since there had been no shared experiences and the students were dependent upon the rather limited provision within the college to gain a sound understanding of classroom approaches. In another instance, students taking English as a BEd second method subject were given much support, but observation of the students' teaching suggested that they were relying heavily on schemes suggested by the tutor or class teacher rather than thinking for themselves. They were becoming well prepared in only a very limited range of methods.

With the exceptions noted, the large majority of courses were helping students to develop appropriate skills through a range of different activities, both in the training institution and in local schools. Institutions will need to consider how the good practice which characterises the greater part of their subject method work can be made universal. This practice recognised that the most effective specialist method of teaching is closely related to general classroom skills such as identifying clear teaching objectives, matching the work to pupils' individual needs, and carefully planning continuity and progression.

Teaching methods used by tutors

The evidence from the survey indicates that in the majority of lecture and seminar sessions in secondary BEd method courses, students encountered a wide range of teaching strategies which they themselves might use. The methods employed by tutors were often good, with lectures well presented and sound in approach, and encouragingly active participation by the students. In only a minority of the BEd courses did the teaching methods fall below a satisfactory level, and for the most part the tutors themselves were actively providing students with good models for their own teaching. For example, in a CDT course the variety of teaching methods included group talks, demonstrations supported by the use of appropriate visual aids, and discussion among the students, who were encouraged to prepare and make their own contributions in the form of demonstrations and short lectures. Similarly, a home economics course employed a wide range of approaches which included the use of micro-teaching and of computer-based teaching.

In PGCE subject method courses, the teaching methods employed by tutors could be regarded in almost all cases as exhibiting good models for the students' own future teaching. Only in a minority of cases was it apparent that the lecturers did not look upon their tutorial sessions as opportunities to demonstrate good teaching methodology. It was to the credit of many institutions that they were prepared to evaluate their teaching in a professional way, and there was much evidence of capable, interesting, and lively teaching. Typically good practice at PGCE level is illustrated by an example from an institution where it was an established principle that tutors' teaching methods should afford students good examples of planning, presentation, and evaluation. In applying this principle, two English tutors worked as a pair with 15 students, taking turns in making the lead contributions. The methodology included lectures, group discussions, whole class discussion, workshop activities, and individual tutorials. A central feature involved students in preparing and teaching lessons and in discussing these with the rest of the group. Illustrative examples of pupils' work were fed in by means of video, tape recording, and photocopying.

In their BEd subject studies, students also experienced a variety of teaching styles, most providing them with satisfactory models, many with particularly good ones, and only a minority with very poor models. In the majority of examples the methods used were considered to be well matched to the students' needs, and in two-thirds of the classes visited the tutors were regarded as providing the students with satisfactory to good examples for their own future teaching careers. In one home economics course, for example, the methods employed in teaching the subject were appropriate and well matched to the students' needs and capabilities, and could be adapted by the student for later use in the classroom. There was good use of the blackboard, excellent documentation, and clear presentation of aims and objectives. For the most part, the students were seeing at first hand what could be achieved when work was well presented, rigorous, demanding, and conscientiously taught. Similarly, in a main mathematics course the teaching methods employed were very effective as a means of presenting the subject, ranging across formal lectures with student participation, practical sessions, seminars, small group work, individual tutorials, and individually guided project work.

Conversely, there was an example where the teaching was poor and the students were overwhelmed with superficial information which they had no chance to digest, and another where there was a great deal of direct lecturing with the emphasis on getting the answer right. Some students appeared to be uncritical of the way they themselves were being taught, and in contrast to their approach to method courses they did not see the connection between their specialist subject work and how they themselves might teach in the future. Even in institutions where the tutors were providing good models, either in the method courses or in BEd subject studies, it was rare to find any explicit discussions with students on the methods which were being employed.

The secondary school curriculum

A majority of colleges addressed the issue of the relationship between individual subjects and the whole secondary curriculum, some implicitly rather than explicitly. In general, however, colleges were not dealing with this aspect effectively, and a quarter of PGCE and about a sixth of BEd courses did not appear to deal with it at all. Where evidence was found of the issue being treated, only half the BEd and a third of PGCE courses were dealing with it in a satisfactory manner. Within individual subjects, it appeared that home economics was most likely and modern languages least likely to deal with this question effectively. Good examples were not common, but a few are worthy of note. In one of the best cases, a PGCE science method course, lectures and seminars covered the 'integrated curriculum' and an analysis of the school curriculum at large. These were related to science 'enquiry' projects involving cross-curricular preparation on topics such as water or transport, and the students were encouraged to explore the relationship of science with history, geography, economics, and other curricular areas. In one institution, a session on 'Curriculum: 14 to 18: An Education for Life' examined curricular issues across a wide range of subjects, while in another a lecture in a course on theoretical studies for all students advanced interesting general arguments about the integration of the school curriculum. Students were then asked in follow-up seminars to discuss how far the themes of the lecture were relevant to their own disciplines. In one such seminar a good deal of generalised scepticism was skilfully handled by the tutor. Another example was provided by a social science course, which contrived to cover the ground through a combination of tasks required of students. During their first attachment students had to report on the place of the subject in the school's curriculum and follow this up in written work; curriculum documents, both official and unofficial, were the subject of workshop sessions, and it was mandatory for these students to demonstrate in their own teaching in schools that they were contributing to the development of pupils' language and numeracy.

A somewhat different but valuable approach was identified in a mathematics course where considerable stress was placed upon the use of mathematics in other curricular areas, including computer applications. The course also contained some reference to the value of mathematics for industry and to the justifications for teaching different aspects of the subject. Here the students were given a good understanding of the relationship of mathematics to the curriculum as a whole, for the course had an outward-looking emphasis. Similarly a BEd PE course encouraged this wide vision through a substantial third year curriculum project, when students attempted to relate physical education to the whole curriculum. They were assisted in this by their second subject, which gave them some familiarity with classroom-based subjects. Good as these examples were, they were by no means typical, and it was more common for the topic to be presented unconvincingly or to be absent altogether. An English course in one of the institutions illustrated this well. Students were introduced to the key notions of language in learning across the curriculum with reference to the Bullock Report[1] and other stimuli, but there was no active exploration of inter-subject links. A great many colleges saw their role as training single subject specialists, and often even the relationships with closely allied subjects were undeveloped. This was clearly exemplified in a science PGCE course, where the question of balanced science in a balanced curriculum was ignored despite the professional currency of this issue. Students were encouraged to see themselves as either physics or chemistry specialists, there were no links drawn between the two subjects, and there was no consideration of biology. Yet many of the students would enter science departments where they would certainly be expected to teach some general science.

Syllabus design

While there was insufficient attention to a view of the curriculum as a whole, institutions did offer the students guidance on syllabus design in individual subjects. Units on the planning of items within a syllabus featured in many courses, and it was apparent that these worked more successfully when tied to specific topics than when the issue was dealt with in general terms. In one BEd course the usefulness of a general workshop on curriculum planning was severely impaired by the selection of examples from the primary field only. In a PGCE course for RE students, a morning was planned on how to design a syllabus, but the session actually concentrated on the planning of individual lessons. Much more successful was a science PGCE course which encouraged team work in the planning of materials for teaching. Students all worked in a simulated science department and had to design curriculum units for a specified age or ability group. This was an ambitious project which was proving of great benefit in allowing students to develop insights into syllabus construction.

Relationships and classroom management

An important characteristic of teachers is the ability to establish relationships with individual pupils and with classes generally. One vital part of the selection of students for teacher training courses is to assess their ability to form appropriate relationships with people and particularly with the young. The course needs then to build on this ability, to develop skills of classroom management and the kinds of working relationship in classrooms where there is mutual respect between teacher and pupils.

---

[1] *A language for life*. Report of the Committee of Enquiry chaired by Sir Alan (now Lord) Bullock. HMSO, 1975.

Quality in schools: the initial training of teachers

The students observed teaching were at various stages of their teacher training course, but in as many as three-quarters of the lessons they had established good relationships with pupils and were controlling classes well, in several cases to a very high standard. One science lesson with 12 to 13 year old pupils of very low ability, taught by a PGCE student, was characterised by lively discussion, encouraging remarks, good humour, and excellent relationships. In a successful home economics lesson given by a BEd student the classroom relationships were based on a very evident mutual respect. The organisation and management of the class were well conceived and were carried out with precision, good humour and common sense, with the result that the student established subtle but firm class control. The student had clearly learned a good deal about group observation, managing equipment and resources, involvement in pupils' practical work, and the appropriate use and management of time available. There were markedly poor relationships in classrooms in only a handful of cases.

It is a matter for concern that students were sometimes given classes where the problems were of such a scale that even experienced teachers in the school found difficulties in teaching the classes adequately. The principle was not always observed that, as far as possible, students should experience the kinds of classes and conditions which will give them the confidence to develop relationships with pupils and skills in class management. Although it is acceptable for them to meet a range of behavioural problems in their training, these need to be accompanied by skilful and unobtrusive support from teachers and tutors. The effectiveness of such arrangements was illustrated by a music PGCE student who was taking a class which the head of department in the school described as 'one of the worst behaved classes in the school'. The performance of the student was to some extent affected by the ebullient behaviour of some of the pupils, but the lesson was well planned, the student was conscious of support, and in general the teaching was effective.

Meeting the individual needs of pupils

The evidence from the visits indicated that there is a disturbingly large number of students who are not being given a satisfactory preparation to help them with these difficult aspects of teaching. Fewer than half the PGCE and BEd subject method courses were providing students with an understanding of the varieties of pupils' needs in terms of ability, culture and background, and helping students to make the teaching of their subject relevant and interesting to a full range of pupils; in only a few of these cases was this preparation of a high standard. In the others, students were not being adequately helped to recognise that the content and processes of learning have to be appropriate to the pupils' level of understanding and previous experience, that they benefit from approaching new ideas through a familiar context, and that they need to appreciate the relevance of what they are learning to their immediate or future needs.

In some cases there had been an attempt at such preparation, but not in a form which helped students to obtain real benefit. For example, in a PGCE modern languages course some of the elements dealt with a range of pupils' needs, and time was spent on graded tests which were used in local schools, but there was little evidence that students were really coming to grips with the issues. In another PGCE modern languages course, the documents referred to the range of pupils' needs but the work in progress related only to the more able. There appeared no suggestion that method, materials and books would need to be varied to suit different abilities. Instead, the emphasis seemed to be on the requirements of the GCE O-level examination. A student on this course was observed teaching in school and he was clearly experiencing many difficulties. In particular he had little idea how to achieve his objectives, since he misjudged the level of the class and seemed ill prepared to teach pupils of average and below average ability.

School visits and teaching practice were potentially valuable opportunities for the students to acquire practical experience of mixed ability classes, but in their own teaching they showed few signs of differentiating work to meet individual pupils' needs.

There were similarly limited approaches to these issues in some of the BEd courses. Typical of these was a method course for mathematics specialists where very little time appeared to be given to helping students gain an understanding of the varieties of pupils' needs that they would meet in their teaching. The course description included reference to children with special learning needs and to mixed ability classes, but little attention seemed to be given to these aspects of the work. Students were made aware of the nature of various kinds of needs, but they were offered little guidance on what actually to do in classrooms to meet them.

Where the practical application of the work had been properly considered, the students were gaining a confident understanding of how to take account of it in their training. A good example was a BEd home economics course which contained elements devoted to special needs, multi-ethnic issues, and equal opportunities. Visiting teachers contributed to each of these topics, describing how they featured in their own work. Practical teaching experience for the students occurred on one day each week, and they were guided towards an understanding of these issues through carefully constructed assessment sheets which complemented their own critical discussion of their experiences. In another BEd home economics course, which made similarly good provision, students were observed using sound techniques of discussion with individual pupils, adjusting the level to the perceived capacity of the child. The less able were stretched and helped appropriately, while more was expected of the abler pupils in terms of oral response, written material, and pace of working.

Among BEd courses perhaps one of the best examples of this aspect of the students' training was in a PE course. In this example, explicit attention was given to the topic of pupils' learning needs in the lectures and, during visits to schools, students were encouraged to observe differences in ability and to discuss them fully. Particular attention was devoted to catering for individual differences in practical activities such as gymnastics or dance.

An example of where students on a PGCE course were being helped to accommodate the range of pupils' differences was noted in a course for drama specialists. Micro teaching techniques were used and there were frequent visits to schools with a full range of pupils. For teaching experience, students were assigned to schools in pairs, a useful and supportive method of encouraging mutual planning, presentation, observation and evaluation.

In a PGCE physics course, problems associated with teaching different ability groups within a class were mentioned regularly in college sessions. In the tutor's notes to students on their lesson plans there was frequent reference to the need to consider pupils of different abilities and whether what was proposed could be tackled by all. The need to suit the task to the individual was clearly emphasised.

A mathematics PGCE course provided several ways in which students became familiar with the range of pupils' needs and how to cope with them. Lesson preparation, a study of resources, and the grading of pupils' work all formed part of the course. Questioning techniques, mixed ability teaching and group methods were discussed, followed by a micro-teaching exercise, and students also worked with small groups of lower attaining pupils. Essential reading for the course included books which provided insights into the varieties of pupils' needs and how they could be met. Students were made aware throughout of the wide range of such needs, and much time was given to encouraging them to make their teaching relevant and interesting, though this did not extend to gifted children. There were courses where staff showed a sensitive awareness of the need to help students develop teaching methods suitable for a wide range of pupils, but there was scope for much more to be put into practice. For example, in a PGCE science course the needs of physically disabled pupils featured strongly, and the needs of girls in science were carefully considered, but the teaching of science to the least able still required development.

In a number of instances, both in PGCE and BEd, the documents indicated that the needs of a wide range of pupils formed part of the method courses, but in reality this topic was being adequately covered in too few cases. In some, students were expected to develop an understanding of these needs and the related teaching skills from their experiences in school, with little related work in college. Indeed, some colleges appeared to rely too heavily upon the careful selection of a variety of school experience as their main strategy for dealing with this aspect of training. Since there was commonly no corresponding work within subject method courses in the institution, the strategy was generally found wanting. In the more successful courses students were considering these issues in relation to their experiences in school, and this practice should be extended. In nearly all cases students could be given more specific guidance on how to plan, prepare, and organise work to match the wide range of individual needs they will encounter in their teaching.

Special educational needs

A small number of institutions had adopted a permeative approach to special educational needs, but the more usual pattern was a short common course followed by options. A few institutions provided options only, and in one case the content of the option was inadequate, with a narrow concentration on remedial education. Another had an option concerned with slow learners, and this focused solely on English and mathematics at the lower end of the secondary school. Arrangements by which attention to pupils' special needs was represented only by options must be considered unsatisfactory, since it was possible for many students to devote little or no time to this essential aspect of training.

In contrast to this kind of provision was that provided by one institution which supplemented the permeative approach with a substantial component compulsory for all PGCE students. This took up most of the education studies programme during one term and was taught by a tutor who had been seconded for a year to gain specialised experience in this field. Students were introduced to such aspects as identifying children with special needs, deciding upon appropriate teaching methods for major curriculum areas, relationships with parents, and sources of external support. The assessment of students was carried out through a school-based case study.

There were a few examples of substantial courses which purported to give the student a specialist strength in this area. One college provided such a course for PGCE students wishing to work with slow learners and to acquire a measure of subject specialist competence through their subsidiary method course. They were required to have gained some practical experience through a school attachment or similar arrangement, prior to entry, and the course itself was essentially school-based.

Variations of practice were also found in secondary BEd courses. In one such course all students had been supplied with a most helpful booklet designed to provide them with a framework for the study of special educational needs within their professional and education studies workshops. The booklet referred them to sections of the *Education Act 1981,* and to reports and books which had particular reference to their specialist subject. They were also encouraged to use the *British Education Index* for their reading. In another BEd course, all students had a compulsory component on special needs within their third year education studies course. This had an admirably practical focus and was concerned with children who experienced problems in social learning as well as cognitive learning. Lectures, seminars and assignments were backed up by packages of teaching material the students could use in the classroom and by booklets written by the tutors. The course was followed in the fourth year by a component which aimed to give students an understanding of the nature of specific learning difficulties and equip them to apply this understanding to developing individualised teaching programmes.

Within the various forms of provision there were some good teaching sessions, both in BEd and in PGCE. One informative lecture on the Warnock Report's recommendations exemplified the value of single session contributed by able speakers. In another example of good practice, students listened to an extract from a DES audio tape of a staff room discussion arising from an incident in which a child with learning difficulties had torn up another child's work. The students then divided into threes, one taking the role of teacher, another acting as the complaining parent of the second child, and the third making notes on the discussion and its outcomes. In a third example, the tutor linked the students' previous experience on teaching practice with a talk from a visiting educational psychologist and a video recording on specific learning difficulties; the insights deriving from each were used to explore some aspects of assessment. These and similar examples showed what could be achieved with sound and imaginative planning. All students should encounter work of such quality and should be enabled to see the relevance of special educational needs to their work in the various parts of their training.

Ethnic diversity

When individual differences were being discussed in any extensive way, differences in pupils' ability figured far more prominently than differences in ethnic background. Some institutions appeared to give little attention to the latter or to the related issue of education in inner-city areas, or treated them only incidentally. One institution which purported to address this aspect of training explicitly in its BEd course had produced a component which had not achieved a proper balance between lectures on social issues and guided practical involvement in school and the community. Students found the statistics being provided about different educational achievements from various ethnic groups of less relevance than help in teaching such pupils more effectively, for which they had asked.

There were exceptions to this general finding, and several institutions were making commendable efforts to introduce students to various cultures and faiths through personal contact. One institution organised an annual two-day conference on multi-ethnic issues for all PGCE students, with follow-up classes in individual subjects. Though the timing was not entirely appropriate and the organisation could have been improved, this was a creditable enterprise aimed at developing students' awareness across a range of subjects. Another institution provided for PGCE students an 'Adolescence Project' which enabled a close study of pupil differences, and this was linked to curriculum preparation for the special needs of a minority of pupils in the context of the wider needs of a multi-ethnic society. In a PGCE drama course there were some outstandingly good teaching practice lessons in inner city schools where white pupils were sometimes in a minority. A particularly interesting feature of the best work was the manner in which students allowed the pupils to translate problems and solutions into idioms of their own understanding and culture. Observation revealed the high quality of the students' perception of drama and their knowledge of its possibilities. In one institution a full-time specialist had been appointed to provide teaching on multi-ethnic issues and build up supporting resources. He and his two part-time colleagues provided a significant contribution in this area to the education studies programme.

Courses in which a consideration of multi-ethnic issues was said to permeate all their elements had variable success. This policy was least successful where the tutors accorded it low priority and where this was sensed by the students. Conversely, it was at its most effective when steps had been taken to support tutors in the various courses and to ensure coordination or collaborative working. A typical product of such organisation was a valuable seminar which took place in an ethnically mixed secondary school and drew upon students' practical experiences in various subject areas. It provided a useful illustration of the permeation of multi-ethnic issues through different aspects of the curriculum, and the course of which it was a part drew upon the help of visiting speakers, including an LEA adviser and members of ethnic minority groups.

Language and learning

Most students appeared to have some introduction to the importance of language and its influence on learning, but something of a divergence between the experiences of BEd and PGCE students was apparent. In many BEd courses the topic was explicitly referred to in course outlines and duly received attention in class tuition and course content. Yet, in general, it was observed that students did not translate this work on language into effective teaching strategies in the classroom. Two BEd mathematics courses summed up the position. Though language use featured prominently in the course description at one college, the students showed little consciousness of it during teaching practice; at the other college, language was emphasised during the mathematics method course but there was little evidence of student-tutor interaction.

PGCE students appeared more likely to have assimilated the importance of language in children's learning. In a large majority of PGCE secondary courses, language in the classroom was discussed in an explicit fashion and treated effectively by students. Among many reasonable examples seen, the following illustrate good practice. In a mathematics course considerable emphasis was given to the way language, as used by both teacher and pupil, can affect the quality of learning, and students were encouraged to use a wide range of precise mathematical language and to develop a mathematical vocabulary. In a modern language course there was an element on 'language in education', and video was effectively used to observe children's use of language in the classroom. This led to an interesting group discussion on the value of exploratory talk among pupils. The same course also included a talk from a teacher from an inner city school whose topic was the language needs of children in such shcools. In a particularly good session on a social studies course, the students were introduced to the role of questioning in class, then divided into pairs and asked to devise suitable questions on socialisation. Several produced imaginative approaches and all took great care with the wording of questions. Each suggestion was subject to critical scrutiny from the whole group and there was to be follow-up television work also involving questioning. In general, the evidence suggests that PGCE students are being reasonably well equipped to understand the role of language in the learning process.

Quality in schools: the initial training of teachers

Personal and social development of pupils

An important element in the training process is the extent to which individual courses point up the contribution which the subjects of the curriculum can make to the personal and social development of pupils. Evidence of attention to this aspect of the work at secondary level was patchy, and although syllabuses and schemes of work sometimes referred to social and personal development needs, these were not often explicitly mentioned in the actual presentation of lectures and seminars. In only a small proportion of subject method courses were students being given a clear understanding of their role in relation to personal and social development, and in two-thirds of cases this aspect was not actually being covered. Occasionally, a correlation between subject method and education studies offered good opportunities for some discussion of personal and social development. For example, in one BEd course the integrated study of PE subject method and education studies was enabling the study of personal and social development of pupils, and this was strengthened further by the considerable amount of time which students spent on weekly visits to schools, community centres and youth clubs.

At PGCE level the choice of content in some subject areas, notably English and history, often lent itself to a discussion of personal and social issues. Thus, literary studies in one English method course aimed to illustrate personal and social aspects both within the texts chosen and in the approach to them. Similarly, in a history course the contribution of the subject to social and personal development received attention, and there was emphasis on the need to involve pupils in discussion and encourage their active participation in lessons. In another institution, social studies was an area where constant reference to pupils' own experience was advocated as an important resource.

The implications of the subject for personal and social development were considered more explicitly in some courses than in others. For example, in one home economics course it was taken for granted that personal and social development was central to the teaching of the subject and it therefore permeated the whole course. In a mathematics and computer course, discussion of the social aspects of children's work in computing helped to make students more aware that their teaching can contribute to pupils' personal and social development. Conversely, a mathematics course at BEd level revealed very little evidence to show that the students were being led to an understanding of the contribution their subject could make. In one BEd CDT (Craft, design and technology) course and some science courses, the consideration of pupils' personal and social development was barely satisfactory. That the needs of personal and social development can be considered on a wider front was well illustrated in a PGCE science course where the caring and encouraging ethos of the department was commendable. Personal and social development was an area which was actively promoted both by the work and by the example set by the staff themselves.

Assessment

Most institutions introduced students to the assessment of pupils' achievement, and about half of these were dealing with it in a satisfactory manner. There were a few cases where the issue was considered in isolation from specific subjects, which impaired the value students could derive from it. In about a fifth of the courses, assessment did not appear to be receiving any explicit attention at all.

The survey revealed that institutions which were dealing with assessment particularly well adopted a diverse range of effective approaches. For example, in one BEd CDT course an introductory lecture was followed by group discussion in which the students reported back on recent teaching practice experience. They were invited to evaluate a form of assessment that had been used on themselves a few weeks earlier. Criticisms from students were handled in an objective manner, and the discussion was conducted skilfully. In another BEd course there was effective use of testing and measurement within PE to assess and evaluate pupils' performance, and this was also strongly featured in a unit on teaching analysis. In this institution, PE students were encouraged to make close observation and recording a regular feature of their teaching.

PGCE equally produced some varied examples of good practice. In a social studies course, the theory and purposes of assessment were well discussed and linked to practical techniques. A number of different methods of assessment were evaluated against the stated aims and objectives of the relevant course. A particularly good feature of this work was that it was coordinated with parallel work in education on norm-referencing and criterion-referencing. Activity in both areas had been jointly planned and this reinforced the effective guidance the students received. In a drama course students gained knowledge of assessment through frequent reference to micro-teaching and through discussions on evaluation. There was a full examination of various models of assessment in the light of the available resources. Good practical sessions were also observed in both history and geography. A group of history students was required to analyse and evaluate examination scripts, and their written assignments indicated that the principles of assessment had been well understood. Similarly, geography students were asked to assess several pieces of work before discussing what criteria had been used. They were then introduced to objective testing and to norm-referenced and criterion-referenced grading and were progressively made aware of the complexity of assessment.

On the other hand a number of reservations must be expressed. In some cases, it was clear that assessment was dealt with only implicitly and that institutions relied on school experience to give students a working familiarity with it. In a few cases, institutions placed undue stress upon a limited range of assessment techniques, which left students with an impoverished appreciation of the wider principles of assessment. For example, some modern languages courses dealt only with graded tests, and one mathematics course concentrated exclusively on the correction of error. In general, even where institutions were training students well in the techniques and principles of assessment, they were inadequately linking these to teaching strategies. On the whole, students were not acquiring a well-informed understanding of the relationships between the two. One mathematics course summed up this situation well. Students were introduced to different forms of tests and to the GCSE, but as an isolated theme, and the relationship between teaching and assessment was simply not developed. It was also surprising to find generally that work on assessment was not supplemented by any guidance on record keeping and on reporting or profiling. These appear to be aspects which institutions have not yet taken up.

A vital element of the assessment of pupils' achievement in secondary schools is the public examination system. It was noted earlier that syllabus design in respect of individual subjects was often included in method courses and frequently discussed in the light of the requirements of the public examination system. Students were receiving an adequate introduction to this system in only about half the BEd degrees and in only a third of PGCE courses. There was an extended spectrum of practice from the total exclusion of the examination system at one extreme to its undue dominance at the other. This variability may be initially illustrated by comparing two BEd courses, one in mathematics and the other in English. In the former, there was no evidence of any attention devoted to public examinations; in the latter, there was over-emphasis, with much of the third year dominated by themes relating to the preparation of pupils for O and A-level examinations and with the work based on the assumption that the examination dictates the content and the teaching approaches. Between these two extremes one science course included public examinations during the work on assessment and made the preparation of test papers part of the planned work. Similar variations were found in PGCE courses. In one music course, the staff believed that current public examinations in their discipline were entirely inappropriate and they therefore concentrated on perceiving music as a practical art based on performing, composing and listening. The students clearly were not being equipped to meet the demands of examination classes in schools. That very point was made by students themselves on a modern language course which failed to offer them any consideration of public examinations. Students quickly became aware of this deficiency during teaching practice. On another modern language course, students were not introduced to the full range of examinations. There was no substantive discussion of examinations at 16-plus, though there had been an impressive session on A-level French. This was conducted by a serving teacher, who stressed the dangers of the 'backwash' effect of A-level and advocated methods which were not dominated by the requirements of the examination. Students on this course had therefore received some guidance on how to approach sixth form but not fifth form examinations; exactly the reverse was true of a home economics course. At this college the examination system was included within an option programme and some students had done a special study on examinations, but the majority of students were inadequately prepared to teach A-level groups.

The variable practice already illustrated should not be allowed to obscure the fact that there were some good schemes and initiatives in operation. One institution took useful advantage of the experiences of a member of staff who was active in examination board work. He was able to give students a comprehensive introduction to new developments in the examination system. Students were required to assess scripts and to consider the construction of examination papers, and the course provided as good a preparation as was possible in the time available. In an art and design course the expertise was recruited from outside, and examination officers and moderators visited the college with examples of work. These visiting teachers illustrated how the demands of the examination need not act as constraints, and encouraged students to relate the syllabus to pupils' need and achievement. A history course devoted five sessions to O-level, CSE and 16-plus examinations and a further two to A-level. The focus of these units was evidence-based work in the spirit of the Schools Council History Project. This helped to provide an antidote to the view of examinations as feats of factual recall. Students on an economics and social studies course were given copies of all the syllabuses from the various boards, so that they would become aware of the content of examination courses nationally, as well as of their regional variations. In this case, the staff themselves provided particularly good models by giving broad treatment to the topic without conveying the impression that all teaching is subordinated to the end-of-course assessment.

These examples of valuable practice stand out in what was a very variable scene. It was wholly typical of this disparity that one mathematics course covered the new 16-plus criteria and considered CSE, while a modern languages course ignored these two and dealt with O and A-level. Two science courses exemplify the variety of provision. In one, the demands of the examination system were deemed paramount and students were advised that restrictions on teaching approaches were inevitable. They were even counselled to dispense with pupils' practicals in favour of class demonstrations as a means of saving time. This was hardly encouraging good practice. Conversely, on another course, examination board staff contributed to work on question design and pupils' work was marked in college. The college staff themselves had examining experience with two boards and were at pains to warn students how the pressures of examination work could lead to a narrowing of approach. This was wise counsel, for students need to be able to prepare pupils for public examinations without losing sight of broader educational objectives. Institutions need to consider whether they are adequately training secondary specialists if they are not effectively introducing students to the public examination system and to the impact it may have upon teaching styles. The evidence in the survey indicates a very mixed picture indeed.

Other professional issues

The skills of teachers have to extend beyond those closely related to classroom methods and the curriculum, important as these are. The survey included an examination of the ways institutions helped intending secondary teachers to acquire the wider professional skills and understanding which they are likely to need in today's schools. Among these are an understanding of the place of the education system in society and of the relationship of schools with parents and with the community as a whole.

Quality in schools: the initial training of teachers

The role of parents was considered in the majority of courses, but the evidence suggested that this topic did not receive any substantial emphasis. In a few, mainly denominational, institutions the significance of the school in the local community was stressed. In one instance the importance of good relations with parents was mentioned explicitly in the college's statement of its philosophy, which referred to the boundaries between home and school as 'becoming more permeable'.

It is a matter for concern that there was virtually no evidence of students being adequately introduced to the place of the education system in society and the relationships of schools with parents and with the community. For the most part, students were ill prepared to accommodate the demands of parents or to adjust to the constraints upon the education service. In one institution a local head talked to students about the place of the school in the community and about the pressures upon it. In one or two others, visits to schools and community organisations enabled these questions to be briefly aired. In the great majority of courses, however, students received no instruction about the school's relationship with the community or about the teacher's responsibility towards the concerns of parents. In one or two cases, the view was expressed that students became aware of the role of parents through their experience in schools, and a handful of institutions made some relevant passing reference to the topic. But only in one case, in drama, was there specific mention of parents when, during the students' induction course, teacher-tutors explained to them the demands parents are likely to make. Occasionally, students might attend a parents' evening taking place at a school when they were engaged on teaching practice, but this kind of experience was random. There appeared to be little liaison between the colleges and the schools to explore how this might feature more regularly during teaching practices, and fewer attempts by colleges to link such practical experience with any related parts of the course.

It is important for teachers to understand the impact of technological developments, such as microcomputers, on society. Most institutions provided computer familiarisation courses for all students, but for the most part these were short, averaging about 20 hours. The courses generally gave students some 'hands-on' experience and an opportunity to see various applications of the microcomputer. They were at their most effective when they were linked closely with work in schools and included the study of available educational software and the classroom techniques associated with its use. This, however, was not widespread, and school-based work was difficult to achieve in courses of short duration. Some of the good examples observed showed what could be accomplished where there had been a careful study of the teaching opportunities the microcomputer offered. For example, in a geography method course, students used programs on routes and population statistics. In a history course they stored and analysed data on the local town from historical source material and used the computer for census retrieval. Examples were also encountered in home economics and in PE, where one course used computerised cameras. One science department provided a good environment for technological awareness by having a complete computer system for its PGCE work. The students were given sessions on computer assisted learning in chemistry and biology, and on the use of microprocessors in the teaching of physics. They also had access to the institution's science research project, which produced programmes for local schools. There were also some interesting examples of music courses which explored the potential of the computer and of electronic instruments for music-making. However, such instances were not common, and it was only in mathematics courses that systematic training in the use of computers was generally to be found. Most BEd mathematics students regularly used computers in their work, and they were featured in all but one of the PGCE mathematics courses. In both BEd and PGCE the work included statistical packages and problem-solving by the use of LOGO[1].

In a few institutions, students were also offered substantial option courses. These aimed to produce teachers who in due course would manage, advise upon, and further the use of computers and information technology in schools. For the majority of students, however, the opportunity was not being taken to explore the possibilities of computers in the teaching of the specialist subject. The computer courses were self-contained, and the application of computers and other forms of electronic technology elsewhere in the students' training was rare. The quality of the students' understanding of computers was influenced by the extent to which these machines were used as part of the learning and teaching approaches throughout the institution.

The world of work received imaginative coverage in only a few institutions. Good practice occurred at one college where all PGCE students had an element on the world of work and all BEd students took a unit relating their subject to industry. Here, two members of staff were involved in the Schools Council Industry Project, and on another PGCE course a week was devoted to an analysis of the project. In general, however, the industrial and commercial relevance of the school curriculum was receiving scant attention. Little seems to have changed since the visits by HMI in 1980 and 1981 to find how students were acquiring the necessary skills to help their pupils prepare for adult life.[2]

Coherence within the courses

The students' preparation for teaching might have been improved further if the various elements within their courses had been more effectively linked and made mutually supportive. This would have helped students to understand the relevance of the issues more easily and increased the range and level of their teaching skills.

PGCE courses varied considerably in the extent to which they linked method work and education studies. Some courses did not even attempt to do this, and only in a minority of the institutions were such links both effectively planned and implemented. Practice was at its most effective where courses had been planned and taught in a unified way and where method tutors included in their element of the course the main educational issues. In one institution units of work in education

---

[1] An interactive language for computer programming.
[2] See *Teacher training and preparation for working life* DES, 1982.

studies and subject method courses were planned in parallel so that opportunities to relate the work were guaranteed, though even in this case such opportunities were not always taken. In other institutions there was a general hope that method tutors would be aware of the content of education studies courses and vice versa, but there was insufficient planning or liaison among tutors to ensure that this was realised. The topic of language provides an example. There was a general consensus about the centrality of this aspect of teaching and learning and it was often dealt with both in education studies and in method courses, but the links between these sources were not always explicitly made.

In the majority of BEd courses some constructive links were being effectively drawn between main subject studies and the corresponding method courses, but in about one-third of the courses there was little evidence of any planning to enable students to understand how these different aspects of their training interrelate. There were fewer links between method courses and education studies, and these were most effective where education and method work were taught together, with good staff liaison and some shared teaching. Some subsidiary courses were designed to cover both subject study and method work and in these courses the associations between the two had been carefully thought out.

There were very few links between subject studies and education studies, but those that were found exemplified some valuable practice. In one institution there were well planned relations between units in education studies and work in home economics on consumer behaviour and household science in a changing society. A strong feature of one physical education course was the linking of the subject study and related professional units with appropriate themes in education studies. In another case, education studies material had been designed specifically to meet the needs of students extensively recruited to specialise in one subject, again physical education. In general, however, such practice was uncommon. An example of the lack of liaison was the home economics course where the subject was taught on one site and education and professional studies on another. Although each was separately well planned and taught, there was virtually no linkage between them beyond what the students could derive for themselves. In some of the topics on both sides this absence of linking was leading to fragmentation and superficiality. Examples were found of courses where tutors drew attention to the method they were employing as offering a possible model for teaching the topic to pupils, or illustrated the work by reference to possible teaching strategies, but in general the specialist subject course was regarded as an end in itself and not perceived by staff or students as being associated with education studies. Where this was, quite acceptably, the policy of the institution, it was important that the methodological aspects of the course should have strong links with both the specialist subject element and education studies.

Standards of students' work

Standards of written work

In PGCE courses the written work produced by students was competent throughout, and in a number of instances exhibited very high quality. It was well presented and showed evidence of the ability to conduct small-scale investigations, draw upon background reading, and organise the material effectively. Standards of written work in BEd courses appeared to vary widely between the individual subject areas and from one year group to another in the course of the survey. At their best they provided evidence of a confident and mature approach and good levels of achievement. In one RE course, for example, the written work was exceptionally good; the students expressed themselves competently and their work showed a wide range of reading and scholarship. Two other examples were provided by home economics courses, where the students showed an ability to conduct individual investigations and evidence of considerable background reading. The teaching practice notebooks of one or two third year students were of particularly high quality. In carrying out a study of a school's catchment area, students had walked the area and taken photographs to illustrate the text. Their work plans were thorough and contained sequenced activities, showing a good grasp of simple research techniques. There were also examples at the other end of the spectrum, where the students expressed themselves inadequately.

Written work produced in specialist subject courses in secondary BEd reached standards similar to those reached in professional and method work. Typical of the best was a main subject PE course where the written work was of notably high calibre and some dissertations were of good honours standard. The range of achievement across courses was again wide at the extremes, but with few exceptions adequate standards within the time available were being accomplished. The competence of students was observed to be improving both with successive intakes during the survey period and as individual students progressed through the three- or four-year degree period.

In practical work, including science, mathematics and drama, there were only a few cases where the work was less than reasonably competent, and in some instances a very high level of practical competence was achieved.

The general level of oral work in both BEd and PGCE was satisfactory, and when given the opportunity for open discussion in seminars most students were articulate and enthusiastic, or had become so by the end of the course. Such opportunities were not, however, universally available, and there were several instances where students were not provided with the experiences which would lead to a growth in confidence. On the occasions when students appeared reticent it was evident that the cause was inadequate preparation on their part or unskilled conduct of the session by the tutors. The best sessions were those where the interaction between tutors and students was lively and productive. PGCE students in particular engaged actively in such exchange and were refreshingly ready to question and challenge, but their opportunities to do so varied from tutor to tutor. In some seminars the students sat passively, accepted tutorial exposition without question, and did not evince articulate reasoning or show independence of judgement. In others they showed themselves able to exercise powers of reasoning and put arguments together effectively, and were ready to question what was offered.

Quality in schools: the initial training of teachers

Standards of work in schools.

During the survey, observations were concentrated on block teaching practice, but various other types of school-based activities were seen. A typical example was a BEd session for the first year PE specialists, where tutor and students worked together with pupils in a primary school, and the carefully-prepared work was supervised. The session took place on one day a week over four weeks, and the teacher in the school commented favourably on the benefits also gained by the pupils from the activities.

Students were seen teaching at various stages of their course and consequently the effectiveness of their teaching is not strictly comparable. Bearing in mind this qualification, about four-fifths of students observed were satisfactory or better, with only two lessons considered to be excellent, both of them given by BEd students. Of all the lessons, in both BEd and PGCE, about one in five were unsatisfactory or poor. External constraints, such as accommodation problems and difficult classes, contributed to some of these weak performances.

As this evidence indicates, there were areas where students required more guidance to improve the quality of their teaching. The general weaknesses, which were often noted even amongst students who were otherwise teaching well, were: the failure to identify clear teaching objectives and record these in a lesson plan; the tendency to identify planning with simply listing tasks or assembling materials; and the lack of match in the choice of content of the lesson or of the teaching methods with the needs of mixed ability groups of pupils. These weaknesses, exhibited in some degree by a large number of students, should be distinguished from the characteristics noted in the poor lessons which were scrappily or superficially planned, lacked pace and variety, and were often associated with discipline problems. The students teaching such lessons were unable, even on a final practice, to evaluate their own performances realistically. It must be open to question whether such students should be recommended for qualified teacher status.

One particular strength displayed by many students was the quality of the classroom relationships they developed. Another was the time and thought given to the preparation of lessons. Although there were reservations about the quality of some of this preparatory work, which was sometimes unimaginative, there is no doubting the hard work that students put into it. To use their planning time more efficiently they needed better guidance on the identification of teaching objectives and on the stages of progression of the work to meet the individual needs of pupils.

Teaching practice files were generally kept well, though the quality of the students' own written evaluation of the effectiveness of their teaching generally reflected their level of competence. Capable students wrote about their work with perception, while the weaker ones made more superficial comments and tended to concentrate on the pupils' behaviour and level of enjoyment. These students were often unclear about the aims of a lesson or were experiencing difficulties with classroom management and control, so that success for them was often measured in terms of pupil behaviour rather than the quality of teaching. Some files contained constructive comments by tutors, urging the students to consider further certain aspects of their lessons or challenging their comments on the evaluation of their own teaching, but there were a number of cases where students were not being provided with this form of help. The growth of teaching ability in students is dependent in large measure upon the extent and depth to which they can assess the learning of pupils, relate it to their own teaching performances, and then plan the next activities accordingly. Consequently, the ability to undertake self-evaluation successfully is essential if the students are to continue to develop their professional skills during their teaching careers.

8   Relationships with schools

Choosing schools

Students training in the survey institutions could expect to work in a variety of schools and with a variety of pupils. The extent encompassed, however, differed with every institution and was largely dependent on the range of schools in the area. The most common practice was for students to be offered experience of teaching pupils of varying ages in schools located in diverse social and ethnic areas. Consideration was less frequently given to the teaching methods employed in the school, the quality of the individual teacher to whom the student was attached, and compatibility between class teacher and student.

Tutors particularly valued long-standing contacts with certain local schools. Such arrangements occasionally formed an explicit part of the organisation of the course, through the designation of 'associated' schools, for example. Clear advantages were seen to arise where the association was based on mutual understanding of aims and methods of teaching. There was, however, some evidence of schools being used out of habit, with insufficient attention to their changing character, and of unexamined assumptions surviving after several years of changes in personnel. Imbalances of experience existed in most areas, and were not easy to redress. Primary students in one large urban area where teaching was typically class-based found little opportunity to practise group and topic work. In another locality, where primary and secondary schools alike were very large, experience of working in small schools was difficult to arrange. At secondary level, it was often found difficult to arrange the placement of subject specialists in schools with a broad ethnic mix of pupils within reasonable travelling distance, particularly where institutions were located in rural areas. The organisation of secondary education within an authority was also found to produce constraints; for example, where selection at 11-plus had been retained in the nearest authority, it was more difficult to provide experience of comprehensive schools.

In contrast, in those cases where an institution located in a town had merged with one in a suburban area, enriched association with schools of almost every type had developed. Students from the city acquired greater opportunities to work in villages and small towns and vice-versa. In a deliberate move to widen students' experience one college, based in a country town, arranged for its students to supervise groups of children from urban areas resident in the college during the holidays, with subsequent visits being made by some students to the children in their own schools. Another used an urban studies centre in East London, where students spent three days each week in school and two in community work. Conversely, it was unusual to find students whose training was based in inner-city environments being intentionally placed in suburban schools, or students being taken to small rural schools if these did not, fortuitously, form part of the institution's normal area. The effects of efforts to diversify experience are difficult to evaluate precisely. There were occasions, however, when specific reference to such experience clearly illuminated a student's written work or discussion, for example where a fourth year study on junior pupils' attitudes to reading had obviously gained much from visits to contrasting schools.

Reasonable attention was thus given to providing students with variety in the sense of the differing ages and abilities of pupils, their social background, and the type of schools they attend. A less satisfactory picture emerged where consistency in the quality of teaching was concerned, and this was true of all phases of schooling, especially for block practice. The evidence of students being restricted in what they could do, by narrow or outdated practice, is too strong to be ignored. The institutions were in a difficult position over this issue, since tutors were sometimes forced for financial reasons to choose one school for their students when their judgement led them to prefer another. They could not require an individual head to place a student with a particular teacher, and indeed a head may for good reasons be reluctant to place students with the same teacher too regularly. Nevertheless, students need the opportunity to work with good teachers employing varied teaching methods, and this was not always provided.

Local education authority involvement in the selection of schools was not widespread. In some areas, a committee including LEA officials and advisers was instrumental in allocating schools to individual institutions, and in a small number of authorities close relations had been established between advisers, tutors, and schools. These led to profitable and regular meetings to discuss current thinking on teacher training and issues connected with liaison between the schools and the institution. The influence of individual advisers was more pervasive, but it tended to be informal and difficult to document. Given the need for the identification of good practice to provide students with the best possible models, there is a strong case for greater involvement of the LEAs, particularly through their advisory teams, in liaison between schools and teacher training institutions.

Clear distinctions existed, particularly between first and subsequent practices, in the size and kind of school and the contrasts they provided with students' previous experiences. One institution took careful note of the students' own perceptions of previous practices, and of their interests in extra-curricular activities and in curricular areas where they would like to gain experience. Particularly careful placement of students training to teach children with severe learning difficulties and slow learning pupils was evident in institutions specialising in these areas. There were, however, instances where criteria of any kind, even at an implicit level, were difficult to detect, or where the only obvious consideration was the number of students a school could take. In one such case an institution used a number of schools of which it had no previous knowledge. Another approached a school to take three students without any preliminary visit from a tutor, even though no students had been placed there for several years and the headteacher had changed. Students sometimes complained of a mismatch between their course experience and what they were required to do in schools. For example, one student had been required during a third year practice to teach pupils with severe learning difficulties, even though he had no prior experience of such pupils nor any training related to them.

The head, or more commonly in secondary schools a senior teacher, was the member of staff most influential in determining the class and teacher the student would work with, particularly for block practice. There were good examples of heads carefully placing students with teachers who could support them professionally and whose personality was likely to complement that of the student. Others were careful to choose only class teachers who offered good models of teaching, though some heads were resistant to this idea on the ground that it could have a divisive effect on staff. In these circumstances teachers were given students in turn: a less than satisfactory arrangement. The quality of information provided by the institution about individual students was an influence, but this in itself did not appear to guarantee effective placement. Instances of poor placement were too frequent, and there were cases of students being placed with probationers or with teachers who themselves were not coping.

In some cases, subject departments within the institutions took particular care over placing students who were training to teach as subject specialists in secondary schools. In such cases, the choice of school was likely to be determined by tutors' knowledge of effective subject departments in the students' specialisms. One school was chosen for drama because former students were known to be teaching in the way the training institution advocated. Predominantly, however, school placements for block practice were made for all phases by tutors with a defined responsibility for school liaison, usually after discussion with appropriate colleagues, such as subject or phase specialist tutors. Few schools had a formal say in which students came to them, beyond specifying numbers of students and the age ranges or subjects available.

The need to find schools to which students could travel daily without undue cost or inconvenience was a priority in most, though not all, institutions. In some cases the presence of suitable schools in the locality meant that there were few problems. More generally, however, the wish to use schools close to the college for reasons of time and finance restricted choice and could sometimes expose students to a less satisfactory experience than the institution would wish. Moves might be made to reduce the effect of such constraints by using buses to transport groups of students.

Information and liaison

Letters and documents about school experience were a major source of information for all schools. Most institutions provided schools with general information and further documentation relating to individual students and the courses they were following. Some was very detailed, explaining the range of tasks expected of students, the development of curricular topics and the organisation of work. Also included, though less frequently, was information about the purposes of the block practice and about work done in the training institution to prepare for it. Documents varied greatly both in scope and quality, and most schools felt that they were satisfactorily served. The documents tended not to be written specially for the schools; the more common practice was for institutions to send copies of course documents or handbooks prepared for students. In at least one case, however, teaching practice handbooks were prepared jointly by tutors, students, and school teachers, which ensured that the interests of each were represented.

Many institutions arranged joint meetings with schools to discuss school experience, and these frequently extended beyond the immediate concerns of teaching practice to include a broader range of issues of common interest. A few followed a regular timetable, with introductory sessions to discuss detail before each block practice and follow-up meetings to consider the outcomes. More commonly, meetings were called when they appeared to the institution to be needed. Where meetings did not take place it was evident that teachers would welcome them. There was no clear pattern of attendance at the meetings. Commonly it was heads who were invited, though there were frequent instances of class teachers being invited also. While their attendance was more difficult to arrange, they were a particularly valuable group to involve in such discussion. Teachers who had attended such meetings certainly spoke enthusiastically about their value. Supervising tutors usually attended the meetings, and occasionally students were present also. In a very promising initiative in one institution, pre-practice meetings were used to enable discussion to take place between class teacher, student, and supervising tutor.

A crucial aspect of relationships between schools and colleges was the quality of personal contact between the teaching practice tutor and the school teachers during the planning stages. Where it worked well, the tutor, the student and the class teacher met to discuss the individual student's programme and the needs of the children he or she would teach. There was also much informal contact between the tutor and the school during the whole period leading up to teaching practice, when the student was making preliminary visits to the schools. In the majority of cases, however, schools would have preferred greater importance to be attached to this initial point of contact with the tutor. Heads identified a number of effects of insufficient pre-practice support. These included inappropriate schemes of work, difficulties of management of particular groups of pupils, and uneasy relationships between student and class teacher. The constraints on tutors were evidently considerable. In order to allow for a preliminary visit they had sometimes to reduce the number of visits made during the practice, and there was evidence that these were commonly having to be restricted in both length and frequency. It was also evident, however, that tutors within the same institution, and subject broadly to the same restrictions, could operate in very contrasting ways, with varying benefit for the students.

There was much good practice in evidence, with class teachers being well informed about the students' degree backgrounds, the nature of their courses, their personality, professional strengths and weaknesses, and areas where further experience would be valuable. It was generally not the fault of the training institution that its information sometimes did not reach the class teacher. Within the same school one teacher was unsure whether a student was following a BEd or a PGCE course while another was thoroughly well briefed. In at least two cases, institutions gave copies of documents to students to hand to class teachers because dissemination of information within the school was defective. There was clearly scope for schools to ensure that the information they were provided with was well used. Many class teachers did not have sufficient knowledge of the students' needs and background, a situation commonly exacerbated by the lack of sufficient opportunity to discuss the student's work with the supervising tutor. There was a widely expressed wish, particularly on the part of class teachers, to receive more information about students and about the role of the teacher in the training of those students. Schools did not regard reading documents relating to school practice as an imposition of extra work. On the contrary, they welcomed them, and would like further advice on the part school might play in the training of teachers. There was a manifest tendency for schools to expect clear guidance from the college, and there is obviously scope for more cooperative discussion of the school's role.

Student preparation for practice

Preliminary visits to schools were almost universally found useful by students. In the first place, these visits gave them information about the pupils they were to teach, the stages they had reached, and the resources available. They met senior and class teachers and learned about the school's circumstances, the community it served, and its academic and pastoral organisation. Many institutions gave the student very detailed guidance concerning the information they were to seek, and often the visits provided excellent examples of planning for the block practices. At least two days were normally allowed for such visits, but a few institutions arranged considerably more. When difficulties arose they were often because visits were made at inconvenient times, but in general visits made in preparation for block practice emerged as a very satisfactory aspect of the students' work.

The survey revealed some institution-based work of very high quality designed to help students in their preparation for teaching practice. This included excellent sessions on micro-teaching, involving the use of small group discussion and video films, and on the evaluation of observation schedules. Advice appeared to vary considerably according to the particular tutors involved. The result was that some groups of students were given excellent help, while others were supported inadequately, with only the particularly able students surviving on their own initiative. There were instances of supervisors making their first contact with the student at the beginning of the practice, and of lack of agreement between tutors on what was required in lesson planning, thus confusing both student and class teacher.

With very few exceptions students were required to draw up schemes of work for series of lessons and detailed plans for all single lessons. How well these were accomplished varied enormously, even between students in the same school, and, while the majority prepared adequately, too many schemes and lesson plans were vague and imprecise. Where schemes of work were inadequate, the most important failing was vagueness. Since students did not always have their schemes of work checked by tutors who were specialists in the appropriate subjects, it was not surprising that some schemes of work were devoid of detail and incomplete even in outline. Where lesson plans were inadequate, the most important cause was failure to identify objectives for what the pupils would learn. For example, students commonly planned what they themselves would do, or what pupils would do, but they did not consider what pupils would learn from the activities. Such plans were insensitive to the needs of pupils both collectively and individually. Time and opportunity were generally available for students to consult tutors in preparing schemes and lessons, but there were also examples of conditions which put students at a disadvantage. Where non-specialists examined schemes relating to a specialist area, they were rarely able to offer detailed comment to improve them. In colleges where schemes did not have to be seen by tutors before the practice, a few students either did not prepare them or produced material which caused schools to express concern at its vagueness. Where secondary students were preparing to teach two subjects, schemes for the second specialism were not always seen by an appropriate specialist tutor. Even where good support from tutors was available to meet every contingency, the students felt doubly secure when able to consult teachers in advance of the practice about matching their plans to the pupils' abilities.

The role of the school

A small number of schools prepared documents specifically to assist students on teaching practice. Such papers described the ways in which it was proposed to help them and suggested activities they believed the students would find valuable. In addition, many provided information in the form of documents written for the school staff, or copies of their handbooks. One paper, written specially for students and discussed with college tutors, stated the duties of members of staff at different levels in helping the students and outlined the variety of experiences which the school expected to offer. The paper supplied details of the experiences students could expect while at the school and described the ways in which members of the staff hoped to contribute to the students' professional development. Documents such as this are valuable in identifying the positive ways in which practising teachers can help students and in indicating the opportunities which only schools can offer. Where such documents are planned they would gain much if developed jointly by school and teacher training institution.

In secondary schools it was common for all students to be placed under the general supervision of a senior member of staff who acted as mentor and organiser of practice within the school. In at least one case this policy was the direct result of an LEA initiative. In primary schools the head or deputy head more commonly fulfilled this function. Where such a policy was established and the college took good advantage of it, the benefits to the student were considerable. There is very little evidence of any training for such teachers, however, and there is scope for the development of structures, support, and in-service training, designed to improve the supervision of students in schools. In the schools associated with at least two colleges, responsibility for students was taken by teachers designated as teacher-tutors. With the active support of their LEAs these teachers worked for part of the week with students in college and for part of the week with the same students in school. This imaginative approach established close practical links between the college-based course and school experience. The examples were associated with serial rather than block practice, but the arrangement is one which could profitably be extended.

There could well be an advantage in specifying more exactly the duties of teachers designated as responsible for students, though many clearly gave strong support on a pragmatic basis. There was no consistency even about such a basic task as constructing the students' timetable. Sometimes it was done by the teacher in charge of students, sometimes by the head of department, and sometimes by the head or deputy. The teacher responsible for students did not always even observe the student teaching, though in general the schools were very conscientious about this, and heads, senior staff or class teachers were consistently prepared to observe lessons and to offer verbal or written comment. Discussion of schemes of work occurred frequently as a matter for the teacher with the closest knowledge of the pupils. There were excellent examples of the influence of able practising teachers on the students' work, through informed comment, seminars, introduction to wider aspects of the work of the school, and induction into the profession. They were providing an excellent model for the development of this role within schools.

Patterns of school experience

As an average across all courses, students spent about a sixth of their total time in schools. The major part of this work was in the form either of block practice or of serial visiting, but there were also school-based assignments of many kinds. For the most part, school experience was well structured for both BEd and PGCE students, with a good balance between serial and block practice. In a number of cases serial attachment in one school was followed up by a block practice in the same school, an arrangement which appeared to be welcomed by students and schools. Many PGCE courses began with a number of days in school in the course of which students carried out a series of generally well planned and detailed observation tasks. In school experience placed early in the course, the training institutions commendably asked schools to give students opportunities to teach small groups of pupils and often, in the case of primary schools, to read stories and observe the use of language by teacher and pupils.

Certain kinds of course organisation required special arrangements for school experience. The DipHE courses in all the institutions which provided them included work experience of one kind or another in the first and second years, which could take place in schools for those considering teaching. It was clearly not viewed as teaching practice, though students were supervised, increasingly by supervisors who had experience of teaching in schools. In some institutions BEd students were taking their main subject alongside students working for other degrees, and invariably the timing of school experience for the former was constrained by the requirements of joint teaching. In some such instances, school experience could be provided only by lengthening the academic year, with the work in schools being placed at the end of the summer term. While the reasons for this arrangement were understood in schools, it was not seen as a very satisfactory time for practice, particularly for those who might be basing career decisions upon it. These included those students who were following a course which enabled them to defer their commitment to teaching. Such students need adequate time in the classroom, supported by carefully planned preparation. The need to give them some school experience was recognised, but in some cases the experience was insufficient in length and inadequately prepared. Students who moved from BA/BSc to BEd courses at the end of the first year usually missed the first year professional component even if they were able to make up the necessary school experience.

Provision for school experience in the fourth year of BEd courses was varied and often far from satisfactory. The main determinant was the placing of the final assessed block practice. In most cases this took place not in the fourth year but in the third. This was because in these instances the course was generally planned as a three-year ordinary degree, with a fourth year added for those students remaining to proceed to honours. Some institutions stipulated a minimum time to be spent in schools in the fourth year but did not always ensure that it was taken up, while others expected students to make voluntary arrangements. Time available could be very fragmented; for example in one institution only one and a half hours each week were allowed for school experience, whereas the students would clearly have benefited more from a block practice. A substantial proportion of time was usefully spent on written assignments which required work in schools, and there were many examples of students making effective use of their time there after they had passed their final teaching practice. Detailed study of particular teaching methods and the development of cross-curricular projects were among such examples. There were institutions, however, with either no planned experience in school or very little. Now that four-year BEd courses are becoming the norm, the planning and distribution of components across four years should take into account the need to develop teaching skills and maintain contact with schools throughout the course.

Patterns of school experience were diverse and no one arrangement stood out as clearly superior to all others. A careful balance of serial and block practice was, however, a feature of all the patterns which appeared to be most successful. The amount of time spent in schools varied very widely. Most BEd courses allotted between 100 and 80 days, but the extremes were 127 days and 50 days, the latter a clearly inadequate allocation. As has been noted earlier, most PGCE courses allotted between 90 and 70 days for school experience.

The allocation of time overall to school experience was satisfactory, though its distribution across the course in a minority of institutions was not arranged to the best advantage. In two institutions, BEd students did not have a block practice until the fifth term, and in another there were only two block practices in the whole course, with students having to choose at the end of the first the age-range in which they wished to specialise. Weaknesses in PGCE arrangements among the minority of cases included two examples of unacceptably low amounts of time in school, a block of three weeks of unsupervised practice at the end of the third term, and a major block practice placed in the sixth week of training, too early for students to benefit fully from it. The proportion of school experience devoted to serial attachment varied from over 2/5 to very little, the average being approximately 1/5, or 16 days. One BEd primary generalist course provided a great deal of serial contact in its first two years, including four separate occasions of one week each. In this course, college and school-based work were closely related, with good cooperation between tutor and teacher. In PGCE courses, serial attachment tended to average some 25 per cent of school-based time, and the variations were not so extreme. In both BEd and PGCE courses, the best kind of serial practice gave students an opportunity to gain teaching skills with small groups of pupils and to match teaching materials to a variety of pupils and situations.

Secondary specialist students appeared to spend almost all their time teaching their main subjects. A few institutions recommended that students spend about one-third or one-quarter of their time teaching their subsidiary subject, but the time spent in such teaching was generally inadequate. Most primary PGCE students embarked on their courses with a subject specialism, but it was rare for this to be explicitly developed as a teaching strength; a few courses endeavoured to provide semi-specialisms in, for example, environmental studies or humanities, but much more could usefully be attempted.

Types of school experience

The major activity of students in school was block teaching practice. For most students school experience began with short periods in school which were progressively lengthened. Typically, students started with a full day or a half day a week in school. In one instance, primary students started by teaching children in the familiar surroundings of college. In others, students and their tutors paid successive visits to a school, working with the same pupils either as a whole class or in groups and allowing each student to take varying degrees of responsibility. The presence of tutor and class teacher working together was very supportive for the students, who were also able to see children enjoying this extended contact and gaining a good deal from the experience.

Most small group teaching was done on serial attachment, during preliminary visits or, for primary students, at the start of block practices. Serial attachment, particularly where tutor, class teacher and students worked together in the classroom, emerged from the survey as a very valuable aspect of training and as one of the most positive features of relationships with schools. Whether it was timetabled for all students or formed part of a particular curriculum course, such experience created the opportunity for detailed cooperative work and enhanced the tutor as a practitioner in the eyes of both students and class teacher. This occurred at least in part because tutors were able to identify teachers sympathetic to the methods advocated by the college, and because more flexible amounts of time were available than was the case for block practice supervision visits. In addition, a number of institutions had micro-teaching sessions designed to improve the students' skills. In a few cases small group teaching tasks, though well structured and enabling students to observe progression, went on for too long, at the expense of experience of whole class teaching. Conversely, for many secondary students the opportunity for small group teaching tasks was limited and could profitably be increased.

During their time in schools, the majority of students found themselves with teachers who were good guides and friends. Moreover, many schools offered additional experience, including seminars with senior staff and opportunities for the students to observe lessons in classes or departments other than their own. Occasionally, students were given opportunities to discuss their pupils' work with the children's parents and in some cases visited their homes. In one instance students looked after school parties resident in their college, which provided them with the opportunity to help domestically and with educational outings. The students visited the school at a later date to see how the work had been developed. Such experiences are valuable and deserve to be more widely available to students in training. Regrettably, there were also cases of schools where students were exposed to uncertain guidance and poor practice, and some teachers did little more than allow their classes to be used.

One ability that many students were failing to acquire was that of catering for pupils of different abilities and interests in the same class. Lack of attention to this was repeatedly evident both in the delivery of lessons and in their preparation and evaluation. Attention was too seldom directed to the progressive mastery of different teaching skills. Certain skills, for example questioning techniques, were often dealt with in college micro-teaching sessions, but there was not enough planned work in schools on tasks such as assessing pupils' written work. In block attachments there was little evidence of systematic strengthening of performance and the gradual enlarging of a repertoire of teaching skills.

For the most part, students were expected to produce written evaluations of at least some of the lessons they had taught. Where these were inadequate, the most important cause was failure to use the experience constructively for future preparation. Some colleges tried to counter this shortcoming by issuing guidelines for evaluations. In one college good use was made of videotape recordings of students' teaching; each student privately viewed her own recording and wrote an evaluation of her teaching, and the tutor then commented on the quality of the evaluation. All students should receive such guidelines and should have their evaluation supervised. It is essential that mistakes be recognised and equally essential that they lead to learning, not despair. In all these areas, which bear so closely on preparation for work within the classroom, close cooperation between teacher and tutor could substantially improve the quality of training for those students who encounter difficulty.

School-based assignments

In education studies and curriculum studies courses, assignments were sometimes set which required work in schools. Some of these assignments proved to be very useful ways of linking college-based study with school practice. In one good example there was a lecture on the importance of encouraging pupils to learn and on means of providing such encouragement. This was followed by seminars, each relating the theme to a different area of the curriculum, and the seminars were in turn followed by visits to schools. There tutors and students together analysed the needs of particular pupils and how these might be met. In another case, students' experiences of teaching physics during school attachments were reviewed in a workshop session conducted by a physics tutor and a psychology tutor. Out of this session topics were drawn for education studies dissertations that involved work in schools as well as academic work. In a third example, students wrote reports, in the light of relevant theories, on their observations of children who were composing stories for younger children to read.

Assignments like these worked best where students were expected to analyse, where staff had thought through the exercise fully, and where there was close supervision. One good idea for an assignment, a study of a pupil's thinking to be made in the light of developmental psychology, was spoiled by lack of continuous supervision. The school teachers were not involved at all; the education studies tutors who conducted the briefing and debriefing sessions in college did not visit the schools; and the tutors who visited the schools were not present at the briefing and debriefing sessions.

A few students spoke of ways in which their psychology studies had influenced their teaching. All students should be able to bring their knowledge to bear upon their teaching; and a good way of approaching this is through well-conceived assignments relating written work to practical work in school.

Supervision

The supervision of students by college tutors during periods of block teaching practice was without doubt one of the most important aspects of training, in that it provided a major link between school-based and college-based parts of the course. It was also one which gave rise to concern. The reasons for this are complex and include the restrictions of time and resources experienced by tutors as well as, in a few instances, low regard for school visiting within the institutions in which they worked. Nevertheless, the evidence of the survey suggests that the quality of supervision is a matter for appraisal throughout the initial training system.

No clear pattern emerged in the frequency of supervisory visits made by college tutors during block teaching practice. In approximately half the institutions where frequency of visiting could be established with precision, weekly visits appeared to be the norm. In two colleges the BEd primary document stated that tutors were expected to visit their students twice each week. In another, where five primary students were in the same school, the supervisor normally spent two full days each week in school. For many students, however, supervisory visits occurred less frequently than once each week. Examples were regularly found of three visits in five weeks, or five visits in eight weeks. Weak students were usually visited more regularly than others and by more than one tutor. Very exceptionally, students were over-visited, possibly through lack of coordination, as in one case where six tutors visited the same student. There appeared to be no consensus even within a single institution, about the regularity of supervisory visits, which often depended very much on the judgement of individual tutors.

Most secondary students, whether BEd or PGCE, were supervised by specialist tutors for their main subject, but specialist supervision of second subject teaching was considerably less in evidence. Exceptionally, where two subjects were closely related, the same tutor might supervise both. Students and schools generally welcomed visits by a second tutor where his or her role as specialist or moderator was clearly defined. Considerable unease was expressed, however, where tutors clearly lacked the experience to supervise in any depth. This situation was particularly noticeable in relation to the teaching of very young children, reflecting the shortage of expertise in this area in many colleges.

No generalisation can be made about the length of time tutors spent in school on supervisory visits. In a few cases, they were able to spend a half-day or even a whole day in school supervising several students, though most visits were much shorter than this, sometimes reflecting limits set by the institutions themselves or the many other demands on the tutors. Visits of approximately one hour were most common, though some were more fleeting, allowing insufficient time to observe a lesson, much less to discuss the work with student and teacher. Even visits of one hour did not allow the observation of a complete double lesson in a secondary school, and restricted the opportunities for discussion with school staff and students. Commendably, there were many instances of tutors making themselves available in college, or by telephone in the evenings, to extend their contact with students on practice.

An important focus for comment and discussion was the student's teaching practice file. With few exceptions, tutors made written comments on the work they had seen which were then attached to lesson notes. In the great majority of cases such comments were supportive and sympathetic, and many were impressively systematic in building up the student's confidence, developing teaching skills, and offering practical advice on overcoming weaknesses. Tutors varied a good deal in their assessment of the quality of planning and the degree of detail they found acceptable, and also in the extent to which they insisted on students following the institution's guidelines. There was a tendency, particularly where students were teaching young children, to concentrate on organisation and relationships, with too little emphasis on matching work to pupils' abilities, the teaching of specific skills, or extending pupils' language. Some tutors usefully drew attention in their notes to comments they had made earlier in the practice, or to the written observations of teachers who had seen students at work.

141

Valuable debriefing sessions took place in most institutions, either with individuals or groups. In a small minority of cases, teachers from the schools used for practice took part, a highly desirable arrangement which for practical reasons was difficult to establish. These sessions gave students the opportunity to share and analyse their experience, and to examine pupils' work and how it was achieved. They were particularly valuable as a source of mutual reassurance. In those institutions where practice took place at the end of the summer term there was regrettably no time for debriefing. It was encouraging to find that colleges were increasingly making an effort to provide schools with feedback about teaching practice, though such initiatives are not yet as widespread as they deserve to be.

Institutions and schools sometimes disagreed about the best ways of conducting the school experience. This was proving an obstacle to partnership in a few cases, especially where students were less than diplomatic as go-betweens. Not unreasonably, supervising tutors saw their main priority as being the observation of students working with children, with a view to advising them and evaluating their work. There were some excellent examples of tutors doing this in the context of cooperation and discussion with the class teacher and senior staff within the school. It was clear, however, that both heads and class teachers would have welcomed more opportunities to discuss the students' work with the college tutor. Where arrangements such as 'area tutors' or 'team leaders' were established to effect general liaison with schools there was little indication that they worked better than more individually based policies; indeed, they could sometimes lead to a confusion of roles. An underlying weakness was the assumption that all tutors would see their role in a similar way, which is directly contrary to the evidence in many cases. Clear guidelines based on policy are urgently required if supervision is to be carried out more effectively than at present.

Assessment of students

Students were usually clear about the basis on which their work would be evaluated, and all received at least some information about assessment. Many institutions had produced lists of headings to be used in assessing students' teaching performance, and some had gone beyond mere headings to give detailed bases for assessment, recording for example whether all pupils or only a few were asked questions. In at least one college there was an admirable scheme, produced in cooperation with schools, in which criteria were published for each period of teaching practice. For example, to be recommended for a pass in practical teaching in the second year a student had to demonstrate six abilities, one of which was to secure and maintain pupils' attention. Generally speaking, students appeared less certain of the role of the school in assessment. One group realised that the head would report on them but did not know whether their class teachers would report to the head. Students need to be informed of the reporting procedures asked of schools by the training institutions, and all schools ought to be prepared to discuss their reports with students.

The decision whether to pass or fail a student in practical teaching was usually made by the training institution, with moderation by the external examiners. Schools were often asked for their comments, which might be taken into account, but it was uncommon for schools to share the responsibility for assessment. A few schools were not asked for reports at all. Others were asked for reports not covering teaching ability but only such characteristics as punctuality. Many schools did not know how their reports were used and were given no information about the subsequent progress of students after their attachments. Some felt their observations were not given enough weight. In short, schools were not the full partners in assessment of practical teaching which arguably they ought to be. Class teachers were particularly uncertain of their role in assessment, a situation which was not helped by the fact that they frequently did not have a sight of assessment criteria in advance of the practice, if ever. This situation is not one which can be remedied by the institutions alone, and there are some encouraging developments, of the kind referred to above, where schools participate in the designing of schemes for assessing students, or where the class teacher, head, and tutor reach an agreed assessment of each student. In general, however, it is another aspect of partnership which warrants closer attention and improvement.

Teachers in partnership

Institutions were increasingly encouraging serving teachers to contribute to initial training, both through participation in the teaching of courses and through representation on college committees. The most successful participation of teachers in work within the college appeared to take place when the contributions of teacher and tutor were complementary. There were many examples of class teachers bringing their detailed knowledge of pupils and their work to bear on such issues as assessment, the matching of work to ability, and general classroom management. In some cases the teachers were formally designated as teacher-tutors, were recognised as such by their local authorities, and worked with students in school and in the training institution on a regular basis. In others, arrangements were less formal but nevertheless brought the valuable quality of immediate experience to the students' work. There were some good instances of teachers giving school-based seminars to small groups of students. For example, three PGCE students on serial school experience in a large primary school discussed the day's work with the deputy head in whose class they were working with groups of children. The students were asked to give an account of the activities for which they had been responsible, and were helped to assess the children's work and decide what should be done next. General issues were opened up through analysing problems which the students had encountered; for example, catering for slow learners in reading and writing, and approaches to teaching certain mathematical ideas and skills. The discussion was skilfully handled by the deputy head, who had observed the students at work and noted the children's responses. Where the involvement of teachers was less successful it was usually because they were asked to do inappropriate things, such as delivering lectures for which they might not be fitted by training or experience. Contributions from teachers are potentially a source of great strength and should be considered by all institutions for inclusion in their policies for relations with schools.

Quality in schools: the initial training of teachers

In almost every institution there were committees which involved practising teachers in discussion of course proposals, arrangements for teaching practice and, less frequently, the assessment of students. Teachers were becoming increasingly involved in the selection of students, and took on a multiplicity of advisory roles on an *ad hoc* basis for specific purposes. It was not always clear how teachers were selected for membership of committees. In some cases they represented outside bodies such as teacher associations or local authorities. In others they were chosen because they were known to the institution, often through attendance at in-service courses, and were broadly favourable to its policies. It became clear from discussion in many schools that the majority of teachers involved with students did not know which teachers were members of these committees, a situation which would be improved by better communication.

In the partnership between teacher training institutions and schools the staff of the former were usually in a position to devote more of their professional attention to training than was possible for school staff. The most profitable cooperation existed when the college had accepted the major role in nurturing the partnership. This meant in practice that individual tutors made it their business to ensure that individual teachers felt they were being treated as professional colleagues. The notion that schools and the teacher training institutions should be partners in the training process is not new. Partnership has, however, often tended to exist at the level of good intention rather than to be realised in practice. More strenuous efforts to develop partnerships have been made of late, and some of these initiatives were beginning to bear fruit, but others were at an early stage and others still hardly embryonic. Relations between teachers and tutors were almost everywhere cordial at the personal level, teachers found great personal and professional satisfaction from working with students, and there clearly existed an encouraging fund of goodwill. This can provide an excellent basis for progress towards the fuller partnership that all seemed to have in mind. This existed where schools and colleges respected each other's differing views and together provided students with useful knowledge of various teaching approaches. If LEAs were to be involved in the exchange as well, an extra dimension would be added; the role of the class teacher, so significant in the whole process, could thus not only be more clearly defined but also more effectively supported.

The methods employed in the survey

When the survey began, in January 1983, there were 66 non-university institutions providing teacher training courses across all the three countries: 56 in England, 6 in Wales, and 4 in Northern Ireland. A sample representing 45 per cent of the total was selected, with 26 institutions from England and 2 from each of the other countries. In order to provide a representative picture, the sample was carefully constituted to take account of as many as possible of the factors which influence the kind of training a student experiences. To this end, the design provided for appropriate representation of types of institution, providing bodies, geographical distribution, varieties of course structure, spread of subjects, and, in the case of England and Wales, a balance between validating bodies. Of the 30 institutions chosen, 12 were maintained colleges of higher education, 10 were voluntary colleges , and 8 were polytechnics. The variation in size was considerable. At one end of the scale was a small monotechnic of approximately 500 students in which teacher training, initial and in-service, was the sole activity; at the other extreme was a polytechnic of 10,000 students with over 1000 on initial teacher training courses. An illustration of the range and the relationship of teacher training numbers to the size of the institution is shown in Figure 6 overleaf. Thirteen of the institutions were validated by CNAA, 12 by universities, and 5 by a combination of CNAA and university, though it should be added that for one reason or another several institutions were in the process of changing their validation arrangements during the period of the survey.

Of the 26 institutions in England, 17 had been involved in amalgamations and offered a range of vocational and non-vocational courses. Four of these were involved in further amalgamations in 1983, and in at least one case some staff were applying for posts for the third time in the same institution. Of the remainder of the survey institutions, 7 had established diversified courses without amalgamating, though during the period of the survey 2 ceased to have any further intake to all or part of their diversified degree programmes. Only 2 institutions had remained as monotechnic teacher training colleges, and one of these had changed completely from secondary to primary training. Primary BEd courses were offered in all 30 institutions, and secondary BEd in 16 of them. Three institutions offered primary BEd (Mencap) degree courses, and 3 others had significant special educational needs components within their primary BEd courses. One institution offered a course comprising three years of part-time study plus one year full-time for the unclassified BEd degree or two years full-time for honours. PGCE courses were provided by nearly all the institutions: primary courses by 23 and secondary courses

Quality in schools: the initial training of teachers

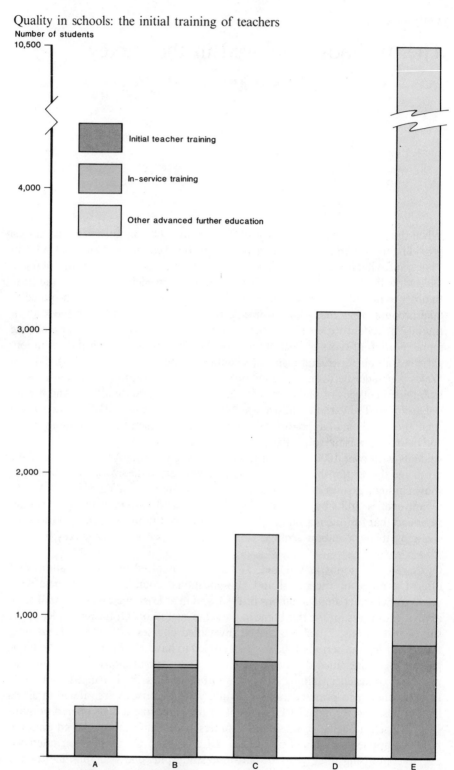

Figure 6 The relationship of teacher training numbers to the size of institutions: five examples from the survey

by 19. The latter covered a wide range of subjects, some institutions offering only one or two and one offering as many as 12. A total of 17 subjects was selected for inclusion in the survey. Fourteen of these were inspected in primary BEd courses, 14 in primary PGCE, 13 in secondary PGCE, and 7 in secondary BEd.

The pattern of inspection differed between the three countries. In Wales and Northern Ireland the institutions received full-team visits for the duration of one single week only. In England, the institutions were visited over the space of two calendar years, with the same group of HMI involved throughout. The purpose was to maintain continuous contact with each institution, and with subjects, phases and groups of students within it, so that aspects of the training could be observed at various stages of the course. All 26 institutions experienced this pattern of visiting, but 16 of them also received a visit by the whole team for the duration of a week at some point in the two years. The pattern can thus be visualised as a continuous scan with a series of peaks. Each team of HMI consisted of specialists in the subjects to be sampled and in education studies, special needs, and primary education. In addition to inspecting their subject in secondary courses the subject specialists had responsibility for inspecting it in the primary phase of training, both in subject studies and in professional curriculum courses. It was the responsibility of the primary phase specialists to produce an overall assessment of the primary courses, and in assessing the curriculum studies and subject studies elements they were able in the case of every institution to draw upon the observations and judgements of at least four subject specialist colleagues, and usually more. In almost all cases, each member of the HMI team visited the institution in at least two of the three terms in each year of the survey.

In total, HMI and Northern Ireland Inspectors spent nearly 4,000 days in visits to the institutions and their associated schools. In the course of these visits, and also during the full-week inspections, HMI attended lectures and tutorials, talked to staff and students, visited students on teaching practice, and read examples of written work. To ensure common practice within the varying patterns of visiting, inspectors from all three countries took part in one another's inspections and worked to the same schedules. Thus, HMI from Wales and inspectors from Northern Ireland joined some of the English teams, and English HMI took part in those in Northern Ireland.

The average size of a team was nine HMI, the smallest number assigned to any one institution being six and the largest twelve. All told, 63 HMI participated in the survey of the institutions in England, with the additional involvement of one from Scotland, who played a substantial part, two from Wales, and four from Northern Ireland. Almost all of the English HMI involved inspected their subject or phase in more than one institution; a number were on five or more teams, and some were on as many as nine. This distribution of specialist HMI across a number of institutions was designed to achieve consistency and continuity. To the same end, leadership of all 26 inspection teams was divided between six HMI, each of whom had responsibility for the inspection of between two and six institutions. This group met eight times in the course of the survey, and there were four residential meetings for all the HMI involved. In addition there were meetings of each individual team at various points in the survey and opportunities for groups of subject or phase specialists to come together.

All the institutions were asked to complete a questionnaire at the beginning of each of the three academic years encompassed by the survey. Visits to the 26 English institutions began in January 1983 and concluded in January 1985, and the 16 full-week visits were spaced out across the two calendar years at the rate of two or three a term. Those to the four institutions in Wales and Northern Ireland took place between 30 January 1984 and 9 November 1984.

The principal criterion which informed all the judgements made by HMI during their visits was the quality of education and training the students were experiencing, in relation to its fitness for the tasks that would be required of them as teachers in schools. All the HMI involved in the survey were subject and phase specialists whose main duties are the inspection of primary and secondary schools, and they maintained these inspection duties throughout the period of their visits to the teacher training institutions. This continuous contact with schools provided for their work in the survey a background of up-to-date knowledge of how teachers were performing their tasks in schools of all kinds. The visits always included assessment of how the students were given experience of schools and how well they performed on their teaching practice. Within their specialist fields, HMI directed their attention to several issues. In the case of the primary undergraduate courses, for example, subject specialists considered the range and depth of the study of their subject, its application to the needs of primary school children, and its relationship to the rest of the course. They assessed its quality in terms of the students' future tasks both as class teachers and as teachers able to offer a special contribution within the school. The secondary specialists posed a number of additional questions; eg were the students led to an understanding of how their subject could contribute to the personal and social development of the pupils, and what was its relationship to the curriculum as a whole? How were the students equipped to deal with the demands of public examinations without a narrowing of content and methods of teaching? By what means were they given an understanding of the application of their subject to preparation for working life and the values of the community? All the HMI involved in the visits observed the range of teaching methods experienced by the students, and the range of teaching approaches the students themselves acquired. The questions to which HMI directed their attention included: how were the students given an understanding of the varieties of pupil need they would meet in their teaching? By what means did they gain a knowledge of the assessment of pupils' achievement and of the relationship between assessment and teaching? Were they acquiring an understanding of the range of educational issues which would bear upon their work as teachers, eg the range of individual differences, background and ability in the pupils that constitute a normal school population, the influence of the use of language, by pupil and teacher, on the quality of learning, the teacher's relationship with parents, education in a multi-ethnic society, and technological developments?

HMI considered and evaluated the students' own standard of performance: their capacity to use oral language confidently and articulately, their readiness to exercise their own reasoning and judgement, the quality of their writing and practical work, and their competence in the classroom on teaching practice. The HMI leading each team pursued with the staff concerned additional questions about the institution's objectives, its policy for staff development and deployment, its resources, and the selection and assessment of students. In pursuing these and many other questions, HMI formed assessments of the work of the institutions and their students across a wide range of activity.

The early sections of Chapter 2 recount the developments which led to the issue of DES *Circular 3/84* and Welsh Office *Circular 21/84*, and to the establishment of the Council for the Accreditation of Teacher Education (CATE). The Circulars made it clear that institutions would be required to submit all their courses to CATE for its consideration, and that in formulating its advice to the Secretaries of State CATE would be expected to draw upon the findings of HMI inspections. The Secretaries of State had earlier decided that all teacher training institutions in England and Wales should be inspected and that reports should be published on each. The inspection of institutions not included in the survey sample began in January 1984, but there was no change of direction in the survey itself. The schedules covered all the issues embodied in the criteria contained in the Annexes to the Circulars, and it was possible to see how far these were already being met without having to frame new sets of questions. Plans to publish individual reports on all the English and Welsh institutions were discussed with the Principals, and the first of these reports was issued on 7 June 1984.

Science and the expressive arts in the training of primary school teachers

Science

BEd

The extent to which BEd students encountered science as part of their professional training depended on whether it was a compulsory element or supplied largely by option. During the course of the survey the latter practice diminished, and by the later stages most institutions provided science or environmental studies as part of their compulsory core of curriculum studies. However, the time allocation for science still varied widely across institutions, and in one instance was as little as 12 hours in any year of the course. Only a brief introduction to science was possible in such circumstances, which was particularly serious where students had little background in science from their secondary school studies.

Curriculum courses included the objectives of science teaching in the primary school, and due emphasis was placed on process and on the features of science most applicable to children's experience. These encompassed observation, description, speculation, experimentation and problem solving. Emphasis on methods of recording was greater for students intending to teach older pupils within the primary/middle school age range. Courses were intended to give students a clear idea of good practice and they did so in several ways. One method was to demonstrate and exhibit as much published material as possible, such as books and other teaching aids used by schools.

Generally, the tutors responsible for primary science curriculum courses in all the institutions were well qualified academically. They were relatively short of teaching experience in primary schools but many were finding ways of acquiring it. The standards of tuition observed were usually good and only occasionally suffered from the inclusion of unwarranted aspects of secondary science. There were few examples, however, of tutors systematically relating work in science to relevant material covered in other parts of the BEd course.

Practically all the courses gave considerable attention to methods of teaching science to children of primary school age. This was often associated with the review of published material and teaching aids including radio and TV. Tutors explained the aims of each selected scheme and displayed selected extracts. Many of the sessions observed gave the students opportunities to try out simple practical exercises so as to judge for themselves the efficacy of the aids and instructions. Because of the large amount of material available, tutors frequently selected a few popular topics such as water, colour, or the (human) senses. This selective sampling was successful with the more perceptive students, who could apply methods learnt in one context to different situations. When science was offered as part of an integrated scheme rather than in the form of single topics, the work involved the examination of part of the environment and its scientific as well as geographical and historical aspects. This approach was set out as a model for adoption in school. It was most successful with students who were already grounded in the essentials of the constituent subjects. Only a limited amount could be covered in the short time available, and much depended upon the willingness of the students to follow up the tutors' lead by careful and systematic reading. There appeared to be insufficient follow-up of this kind, and there was also a need for more preparation. Consequently, although some of the sessions observed were excellent in themselves they were isolated from related scientific study and from any wider work.

Practical work in curriculum courses usually took place in general-purpose rooms or laboratories, and there were few well furbished primary bases which afforded realistic environments to prepare students for the working conditions of a primary school. However, students gained much of their knowledge of teaching method from their school experience, and due reference was made to this by many tutors. In more than half the professional courses seen, the students were gaining an understanding of an appropriate range of teaching approaches. In the rest the range was limited or the treatment was rather superficial.

Though the quality of much of the work was sound, students were seldom helped to develop a view of the place of science within the primary curriculum as a whole, and this aspect needed greater emphasis. Students learned to select material which would interest the children, but they needed more guidance in adapting it and in choosing teaching approaches relevant to the full range of pupils found in ordinary classes.

In general, the treatment of assessment in science was at an introductory level. Students were expected to evaluate lessons given during teaching practices, and a few courses included assignments which required the students to plan work for a group of children, to teach it, and to assess the children's response. In a few cases only were there references to the work of the Assessment of Performance Unit (APU).

The written work required of students often had immediate relevance and practical value. For example, students were asked to produce a set of workcards on a given topic which could be used and evaluated in the classroom. In the main these were well done, but a number concentrated much more on the lettering, colouring and art work than on the science involved. Too many of these assignments were insufficiently challenging to the students and paid little attention to the ways in which pupils acquire their knowledge and skill in science; a matter which presents a taxing challenge to students who lack a sound scientific understanding. Despite these difficulties, there were encouraging examples on teaching practice of lessons taught by non-scientists as well as by those taking a science main subject. A music student, for example, realised that her class of nine year old pupils was confused about melting and dissolving. She clarified the use of both words skilfully and invited the children to speculate about the melting points of a few common substances and devise ways of testing their ideas. This led to a simple practical investigation to which all the pupils contributed. This was done on the initiative of the student, following the general guidance given on science curriculum courses in college. This lesson contrasted with many that were characterised by much initial activity which stimulated interest but produced few worthwhile outcomes. These provided little for the pupils to carry forward into further work in science. Generally, the students were better at initiating enquiry than drawing out conclusions, a criticism that could also be made of some of the teaching they received, which concentrated more on problems than on solutions.

Some of the work in science contributed significantly to the wider perspectives developed by the BEd course. For example, many science courses emphasised the relationship between language and learning and gave concrete expression to it. A number included experience in using microcomputers, and two colleges linked science and simple technology through practical problem-solving activities.

For students who were not science specialists the time available, even in a four year course, was seldom enough to overcome their inhibiting ignorance of subject matter. Though there was some good teaching during school practices, many students retained an understandable anxiety about their own knowledge and competence in science and this reduced their effectiveness in the classroom. Curriculum courses could not supply sufficient knowledge of the subject as well as of the methods of teaching it. This constraint would be eased if these courses had closer links with other elements of the degree, particularly those which deal with the process of learning and children's conceptual development. Much of the work tended, even when at its best, to isolate rather than integrate science, and the value of the training would be enhanced by explicitly demonstrating the place of science within the primary curriculum as a whole.

PGCE

An introduction to science teaching was a common feature of postgraduate courses. The work was generally planned on the assumption that the students would begin with little knowledge of science, since they came with a wide range of degree backgrounds, few of them in science. Only two or three of the institutions provided a separate course for science graduates, one of them catering for just five students. As in some BEd courses, science was sometimes offered as part of environmental studies. In whatever form science was presented, time was a severe constraint. A total of 15 hours was not uncommon and it gave little opportunity to prepare class teachers adequately. The content was similar to that for BEd curriculum courses but the scope was reduced.

Science and the expressive arts in the training of primary school teachers

The qualifications and experience of the staff teaching the postgraduate courses were similar to those described for the BEd. In almost half the courses some of the work was related to other parts of the course. The closest links were with history and geography, where science formed part of an environmental studies course. One or two examples were noted of work done in language courses being taken up and reinforced in science, but there was only one example of science being systematically related to several parts of the PGCE as a whole.

As in the BEd, the teaching methods employed by many of the lecturers provided good models for intending teachers. Students were generally introduced to an appropriate range of teaching approaches for use in schools, often through the study of published material but also through talks and by example. In several cases not enough ground was covered, sometimes owing to the shortage of time, and in others students were dependent on what they were able to gain from general curriculum courses and school experience.

The students generally received sound advice on ways of selecting material and making it interesting and relevant for average pupils, but few of the courses gave sufficient attention to ways of catering for the full range of ability and needs found in an ordinary class. Where the issue was raised it was in practical sessions and when discussing the suitability of published materials for specific age groups.

Consideration was usually given to the place of science within the primary curriculum as a whole, and this was reinforced where science was studied as part of a wider grouping such as environmental studies. However, there was seldom sufficient concentration on the contribution science can make to promoting the development of knowledge, concepts, skills and attitudes which can be put to use in many other areas of the curriculum.

There was equally a lack of explicit attention to levels of expectation and assessment techniques, including less formal methods such as observing how children tackle an assignment, listening carefully to their comments, questions and explanations, and analysing their writing. In a few course outlines there was no reference at all to assessment, though it appeared implicit in what was taught and the general topic may have been dealt with elsewhere in the course. One course gave a sound introduction to assessment, within the constraints of the time available, but in general the topic was under-emphasised.

Many graduates in arts or humanities, and BEd undergraduates who dropped science at or before the age of 16, found primary science difficult. They were anxious about their lack of understanding and their ability to master the subject sufficiently to teach science effectively to their young pupils. Such students were faced in their curriculum courses with a dual task: to learn some science and to learn how to teach it. A typical situation observed was that of students who, at the beginning of a session, knew nothing about electric currents and circuits and were asked to try out and evaluate a set of workcards and instructions on batteries and bulbs. Some of the students were pleased to have an opportunity to learn about electricity but could not decide upon the best method of teaching the subject to young pupils; there was no time for them to digest ideas and redirect their thoughts. Ignorance of the facts of elementary science is not the fault of the colleges, but its implications for their work should be faced squarely. Many of the exercises and examples of primary science seen in college and school rest upon principles which, though simple to the initiated, have to be learned by non-specialists before they can attempt to teach them. Generally, insufficient attention was paid to developing in students an understanding of the underlying principles of simple science.

Expressive arts

BEd

All but one of the institutions required students to take a curriculum course in the area of the expressive arts. Sometimes students chose one subject such as music or art and design; in other cases they followed an integrated course which included elements of several subjects, for example art, dance, drama and music. The majority of the single subject courses were allocated about 20 hours of contact time, but the range was from 7 to 30 hours. A few institutions offered additional optional courses ranging from 10 to 60 hours. Integrated courses tended to be longer, but the attention given within them to the component subjects varied. For example, in a creative arts course of 100 hours, approximately 40 hours were spent on integrated work, but the remaining time was shared out unevenly among the subjects represented; this resulted in the students being ill prepared in some of them.

In some of the art courses the content was sound and well selected, but owing to the limited time made available it dealt with only a very restricted range of the knowledge and skills required by a competent class teacher. Several of the music courses were too theoretical and bore little relationship to the needs of the students, namely a grounding in basic skills and understanding of the range of approaches to music making with primary age children. Integrated courses often sought to combine aesthetic appreciation and expression with knowledge of the constituent subjects. For example, the aims for one course included an understanding of how to help children express themselves creatively; an insight into ways in which creative and expressive activities can stimulate and enrich children's all round development at each stage in the primary school; and personal experience for the students in the separate subject elements within the integrated course. Some of these courses provided a useful foundation for class teachers. Others, for example where the students simply took each constituent subject in turn, lacked coherence, and none of those attempting to cover the whole expressive arts area achieved a satisfactory integration of subject matter and teaching methods. Some courses concerned with single subjects, or small combinations of subjects, were more successful, often pruning their objectives to fit the limited time available.

Many staff were academically well qualified in their respective subjects, some exceptionally so. Most courses were taught by specialists, the other by tutors from education departments and, in one subject area in one college, by a local education authority specialist adviser. Few tutors had recent substantial primary experience, but in several institutions staff were obtaining first-hand experience in primary schools or were in process of arranging it. The general lack of primary background had some implications for course relevance, the methodology employed, and the nature and presentation of the experiences offered to students.

Tutors used a variety of methods to help the students to understand a reasonable range of teaching approaches for use in primary schools. Those students who were taking one of the performing arts in specialist subject studies generally had sufficient confidence in their own performance to learn from observing the teaching approaches used by tutors and by their fellow students. Those with limited previous experience, however, often lacked confidence and did not appear to acquire the insights necessary to teach the arts creatively. These students were helped by courses which emphasised the types of work they could do with children but did not depend on well developed specialist skills. For example, it was made apparent in one music course that while instrumental competence is essential for some primary teachers there is much that others can achieve with an understanding of the content and methods of teaching which does not depend on this particular skill. It was clear that students needed to overcome inhibitions about their own creative abilities if they were to teach effectively, and this required considerably more opportunity than was provided for them to experience, practise, and understand the arts.

In general, the tutors' own teaching styles provided good models for the students. The range of approaches they employed gave the students experience of learning in ways which were appropriate for adults but also had relevance for work in schools, though some tutors did not take sufficient account of the students' needs and previous experience. Inevitably, in the performing arts, tutors were closely involved in the work and most achieved a good balance between direction and guidance. Similarly, in other activities, tutors were conscious not only of the need to provide accurate information and to demonstrate processes, but also to allow the students to explore and experiment. In one music course the initial session on the role of music in the curriculum was given by a local teacher who had considerable success in arousing the students' interest and enthusiasm. Many tutors demanded the highest technical competence that students could offer within the course structure, and most staff created good learning environments in which students were able to respond with enthusiasm. In certain courses, the major weaknesses were the limitation of content and a tendency for staff to over-lecture and to dominate discussion groups.

Little consideration appeared to be given in the curriculum courses to the varieties of pupils' need which students will meet in their teaching. There was insufficient attention to the differences within age bands, and little evidence to suggest that aspects such as concentration spans, manipulative difficulties, behavioural problems, learning difficulties or exceptional talent formed any part of the presentations.

It is understandable that those teaching within a curriculum area made up of a

155

number of subject components should focus on the interrelationships within the curriculum area rather than those beyond it, and this was the case in practically all the courses seen. There were very few examples where tutors explored the relationship between the subject and the rest of the primary school curriculum. In one such example, a music tutor worked with those teaching other subjects on themes and projects designed to show how music could be related to other curricular areas. However, this issue was neglected in most performing arts courses. It was rare to find work in the expressive arts systematically related to other parts of the BEd, though sometimes rather tenuous links were made with child development in education studies.

Although attention to assessment procedure was evident in several courses, their systematic use in schools was not sufficiently considered. Much more attention could be given to the diagnostic use of assessment and its application to learning and teaching, pupils' self-assessment, evaluation, the grading of performance, and systems of recording and reporting pupils' progress. Tutors need to identify more clearly for their students relevant criteria and the methods by which assessment in the creative arts can be achieved. An interesting example of such guidance was where a tutor who had worked on the assessment of practical drama made good use of his knowledge in discussing the relationship between assessment and teaching.

The students' work in some courses was outstanding, but in others the students were being insufficiently challenged and were not given enough opportunities to develop the skills of independent learning. New technologies appeared to form only a marginal part of students' experiences, and reference to the use of computers was made in only one college. Increased use of video tape-recorders, film, slides and overhead projectors could improve the presentation of lectures and enhance the work carried out by the students. The quality of students' writing varied considerably. Essays ranged from reproduced information to the presentation of well informed opinion and argument. Where students were expected to maintain journals, these ranged from straightforward records of events with little personal evaluation to detailed private diaries which included drawings, photographs, the visual recording of objects, written descriptions of ideas, and the exploration and expression of feelings. Many students were articulate in presenting their own points of view in conversation, in group discussion, and in teaching sessions.

Most students who followed specialist subject studies in the expressive arts, supported by relevant curriculum courses, were adequately prepared for work in this area as class teachers. A few were equipped, through a combination of a specialist subject study and a linked curriculum course, to offer one of the creative arts, such as drama, as a curriculum strength which could lead to a curriculum leadership role. However, no examples were seen of students whose preparation would have enabled them to take such a role across the expressive arts as a whole without considerable extra study. Many of the students without a background of specialist subject study were ill equipped for the tasks that would face them as class teachers: generally they would be able to make a useful contribution in music, art and craft, but few had sufficient confidence in dance and drama to be able to teach these subjects without considerable encouragement and support in their first post. This reflects the inadequate provision for the expressive arts in virtually all the institutions.

PGCE

The majority of the PGCE students came to curriculum courses in the expressive arts with a very limited background, many having had no contact with the subjects represented since the third year of their secondary schooling. Those who had studied one of the expressive arts tended to have a relatively narrow view of their subject and often failed to appreciate the breadth of experience which needs to be offered to young children. The time allocation for curriculum courses varied considerably, ranging from less than 20 hours for an expressive arts course comprising arts, drama and music, to a single subject curriculum course of 27 hours. In most cases students training to teach the younger age groups received slightly more time than those training for the older age groups.

The qualifications and experience of staff teaching the PGCE were similar to those of the BEd tutors. Their teaching methods generally provided appropriate models for intending teachers and, in the main, good use was made of the limited time available. However, as noted in the case of the BEd, the range of knowledge and skills which could be covered in the allotted time was narrower than is desirable for a class teacher who is required to teach all the subjects encompassed by the expressive arts. Tutors leading the integrated courses tried to ensure that students understood the interrelationships between the different elements. Consideration was given in some courses to the place of expressive arts in the primary curriculum, but further work was often needed on the specific contribution it can make. In some cases, links were established between the expressive arts and other parts of the PGCE but these could have been developed much more effectively, to the mutual benefit of the expressive arts in particular and the PGCE in general.

As in the BEd curriculum courses, insufficient attention was given to ways of catering for the full range of ability and experience which students will encounter among children in ordinary classes. Similarly, the treatment of assessment and of such issues as the needs of a multi-ethnic society and pupils with special needs was often rudimentary or non-existent.

Students on courses in the expressive arts were often strongly committed and produced work of a generally sound quality, some of it surprisingly good given the very limited time available. In one or two instances where students had a degree in a specific subject, such as music, they had acquired a curricular strength as a result of their expressive arts course and were ready to move gradually towards a consultancy role in a primary school. As in BEd, the constraint of time posed a big problem. Some of the longer courses gave the students sufficient assurance to make a start as class teachers, but the shorter courses were insufficient to equip the students to teach confidently all the subjects in the expressive arts area. Nevertheless, further

157

consideration needs to be given to the time allocated for expressive arts if students are to be satisfactorily prepared to teach this important area of the primary school's curriculum.

Printed in the UK for Her Majesty's Stationery Office by Linneys Colour Print
Dd 239891 C50 4/87